100 DAYS OF INTENSE BODYBUILDING TRAINING AND VEGAN MEALS

SECOND EDITION

GREAT BODYBUILDER WORKOUTS WITH EVERYDAY VEGAN NOURISHMENT

Mariana Correa

Copyright Page

2018 100 DAYS OF INTENSE BODYBUILDING TRAINING AND VEGAN MEALS SECOND EDITION

ISBN

Acknowledgement

To my family, thank you for always believing in me.

About the author

Mariana Correa is a certified sports nutritionist and former professional tennis player. Mariana reached a career high of 26 in the world in juniors with wins over Anna Ivanovich (former #1 WTA in the world) and many other top 100 WTA players.

She competed successfully all over the world in over 26 countries and hundreds of cities including in London for Wimbledon, Paris for the French Open and in Australia for the world championships. She also represented Ecuador in Fed Cup, where the team reached the finals in their group.

During her career she was awarded the fair play award many times, proving to be not only an excellent player, but also a role model for other athletes.

Being an athlete herself she understands what it takes to be the best in what you love.

Mariana is a certified sports nutritionist with years of experience in proper nutrition and hydration for high performance athletes.

She combines her love and knowledge in sports and nutrition in this book to provide you with all the information you need to succeed.

Description

100 DAYS OF INTENSE BODYBUILDING TRAINING AND VEGAN MEALS is exactly what you need to get to the body you always dreamed of, no useless pictures or boring explanations, just the best workouts and nutrition to make you the ultimate version of yourself.

100 Awesome Bodybuilding Workouts that will help you:

- Boost your Metabolism
- Have Six Pack Abs
- Burn Body Fat
- Build some Seriously Strong Arms
- Gain Muscle Definition
- Increase Muscle Mass
- Achieve the body you Always dreamed of

100 days of Vegan Meals Plans. A Vegan diet is great to prevent muscle fatigue and inflammation, accelerate muscle recuperation and improve your overall health.

Every day includes vegan breakfast, lunch, dinner and snacks each of these include a nutritional breakdown of how much fat, protein, carbohydrates, fiber and calories you will be consuming.

50 Bodybuilding Tips. From recovery, nutrition, to workout advice , you will be on the road to the body and health you seek.

The author Mariana Correa is a former professional athlete and certified sports nutritionist that competed successfully all over the world. She shares years of experience both as an athlete and a coach bringing a priceless perspective.

Table of Contents

Acknowledgements

About the author

Description

Introduction: Perfection

Chapter 1: Body Enhancement

Chapter 2: Strength from Within

Chapter 3: Bodybuilding Tips

Introduction

Perfection

"Most people have no idea how amazing their body is designed to perform" Mariana Correa

Let's begin by understanding your body is perfection. Yes, no matter what you think it's perfect. Every single cell works together in synchronicity allowing you to be healthy and perform your everyday activities and training.

An active lifestyle combined with good nutrition is the best way to stay healthy.

Yes, it's absolutely necessary to have a great training program and without it you won't accomplish much, but any champion can tell you that the single most important factor in creating the ultimate body is a proper nutrition plan.

Train hard, eat clean and see the amazing results your body will produce at the end of this 100 day program.

Chapter 1:
Body Enhancement

Focus on working on the correct form on each exercise to get the maximum out of each exercise. Challenge your mind and your body even when you feel like you can't achieve your goal, keep training hard and every day you will be one step closer.

Feel free to adapt the workouts to push yourself harder or take it down a notch if you're not feeling well, the last thing you want is to get injured and have to miss a workout. Listen to your body, the key is to continue to work through every day to see the difference at the end of this 100 day awesome program.

"The Best project you'll ever work on is YOU!"

Day 1   reps/sets

Biceps, triceps, and forearms:

Barbell curls	10/4
Hammer curls	10/4 (Each arm)
Lying cable curls	15/3
Skull crushers	10/6
Bench dips	20/5
Dumbbell reverse curls	10/5 (Each arm)

Keep your upper arms stationary on all exercises , only your forearms should be moving, except on bench dips. Rest 15 seconds between sets and 30 seconds between exercises.

Day 2 reps/sets

Traps and shoulders

Military press   5/3

Dumbbell front raises 10/5

Dumbbell lateral raises 10/5

Dumbbell bent over lateral raises 10/5

Barbell shrugs   15/4

Dumbbell shrugs   20/2

Go heavy on barbell shrugs, and avoid swinging on front, lateral and bent over raises. Rest 25 seconds between sets and 45 seconds between exercises, except on military press, where you should rest 45 seconds between sets and 1 minute and 30 seconds between exercises.

Day 3 reps/sets

Legs

Back Squat   5/3

Leg extension   12/5

Romanian deadlift 10/5

Seated calf raise   15/5

Keep your back straight on back squats and romanian deadlifts. Use a proper amount of weight on all exercises. Rest 25 seconds between sets and 1 minute between exercises on all exercises, except on back squats, where you should rest 45 seconds between sets and 1 minute and 30 seconds between exercises.

Day 4 reps/sets

Chest and back

Bench press 5/3

DB bench press 10/5

Mid Cable crossovers 10/8

Deadlift 5/3

Straight arm pulldowns 15/4

Barbell bent over row 10/5

Keep your back straight on deadlifts. Use a proper amount of weight on all exercises. Rest 30 seconds between sets and 1 minute between exercises, except on bench press and deadlifts, where you should rest 1 minute between sets and 1 minute and 30 seconds between exercises.

Day 5 reps/sets

Abs

Sit ups   15/3

Hanging knee raises 10/4

Crunches   10/3

Keep your torso steady as possible on hanging knee raises. Rest 15 seconds between sets and 25 seconds between exercises.

Day 6

Rest day

Use this day to recover from your workouts. This doesn't mean that you should lie on the couch whole day without doing anything. Begin with a light warm-up, following by a stretch all of the muscles which you have trained, including triceps, chest, abs, biceps, traps, lats, calves, quadriceps, hamstrings, glutes, delts, and your wrist flexors. These recovery days are crucial to the development of your muscle, in order to grow and rebuild, they need time to recuperate.

Day 7 reps/sets

Biceps triceps and forearms

Barbell curls 10/5

Hammer curls 10/4 (Each arm)

Lying cable curls 15/4

Skull crushers 15/4

Bench dips 30/3

Dumbbell reverse curls 15/4 (Each arm)

Keep your upper arms stationary on all exercises , only your forearms should be moving, except on bench dips. Rest 20 seconds between sets and 35 seconds between exercises.

Day 8 reps/sets

Traps and shoulders

Military press   5/3 +2.5kg or 10/2

Dumbbell front raises 12/5

Dumbbell lateral raises 12/5

Dumbbell bent over lateral raises 12/5

Barbell shrugs   10/6 +5kg or 20/3

Dumbbell shrugs   25/2

Add 2.5kg to your military press, and 5 kg to your barbell shrugs. If you can't perform most of the reps with proper form, do as instructed and go heavier on your next workout. Avoid swinging on front, lateral and bent over raises. Rest 25 seconds between sets and 45 seconds between exercises, except on military press, where you should rest 45 seconds between sets and 1 minute and 30 seconds between exercises.

Day 9 reps/sets

Legs

Back Squat   5/3 +2.5kg or 10/2

Leg extension   15/4

Romanian deadlift 15/3

Seated calf raise   20/4

Add +2.5 kg to your back squat. If you can't perform 5 reps with increased weight, do as instructed and increase the weight on your next workout. Keep your back straight on back squats and romanian deadlifts. Rest 35 seconds between sets and 1 minute between exercises, except on back squats, where you should rest 1 minute between sets and 1 minute and 45 seconds between exercises.

Day 10 reps/sets

Chest and back

Bench press   5/3 +2.5kg or 10/2

DB bench press 10/5

Mid Cable crossovers 15/6

Deadlift   5/3 +2.5kg or 10/2

Straight arm pulldowns 10/5 +5kg or 20/3

Barbell bent over row   15/4

Keep your back straight on deadlifts. Add 2.5 kg to your bench press and deadlift, and 5 kg to your straight arm pulldown. If you can't perform most of the reps properly with increased weight, do as instructed and go heavier on your next workout. Rest 30 seconds between sets and 1 minute between exercises, except on bench press and deadlifts, where you should rest 1 minute between sets and 1 minute and 45 seconds between exercises.

Day 11 reps/sets

Abs

Sit ups   15/4

Hanging knee raises 15/3

Crunches   12/3

Keep your torso steady as possible on hanging knee raises. Rest 10 seconds between sets and 20 seconds between exercises.

Day 12 reps/sets

Rest day

Use this day to recover from your workouts. This doesn't mean that you should lie on the couch whole day without doing anything. Stretch all of the muscles which you have trained, including triceps, chest, abs, biceps, traps, lats, calves, quadriceps, hamstrings, glutes, delts, and your wrist flexors to boost out recovery.

Day 13 reps/sets

Biceps triceps and forearms

Barbell curls	12/5
Hammer curls	10/4 (Each arm)
Lying cable curls	10/4 +5kg, or 20/3
Skull crushers	10/4 +2.5 kg or 20/3
Bodyweight dips	10/5
Barbell reverse curls	10/5 +2.5kg or 20/3 (Each arm)

Add 2.5 kg to your skull crushers and barbell reverse curls, and 5 kg to your lying cable curls. If you can't perform most of the reps with proper form, do as instructed and increase the weight on your next workout. Keep your upper arms stationary on all exercises, only your forearms should be moving, except on dips. Rest 25 seconds between sets and 35 seconds between exercises.

Day 14 reps/sets

Traps and shoulders

Military press   5/3 +2.5kg or 10/2

Dumbbell front raises 15/5

Dumbbell lateral raises 15/5

Dumbbell bent over lateral raises 15/5

Barbell shrugs   10/6 +5kg or 20/3

Dumbbell shrugs 10/5 with heavier dbs.
              or   20/4

Add 2.5kg to your military press, 5 kg to your barbell shrugs, and switch to heavier dbs. on dumbbell shrugs. If you can't perform most of the reps with proper form, do as instructed and go heavier on your next workout. Avoid swinging on front, lateral and bent over raises. Rest 30 seconds between sets and 45 seconds between exercises, except on military press, where you should rest 45 seconds between sets and 1 minute and 30 seconds between exercises.

Day 15 reps/sets

Legs

Back Squat   5/3 +2.5kg or 10/2

Leg extension   10/4 +5kg or 20/3

Romanian deadlift 10/4 +5kg or 20/3

Seated calf raise   25/4

Add +2.5 kg to your back squat, and 5 kg to your leg extension and romanian deadlift. If you can't perform most of the reps properly with increased weight, do as instructed and increase the weight on your next workout. Keep your back straight on back squats and romanian deadlifts. Rest 35 seconds between sets and 1 minute between exercises, except on back squats, where you should rest 1 minute between sets and 1 minute and 45 seconds between exercises.

Day 16 reps/sets

Chest and back

Bench press   5/3 +2.5kg or 10/2

DB bench press 12/5

Mid Cable crossovers 10/6 +5kg or 20/4

Deadlift   5/3 +2.5kg or 10/2

Straight arm pulldowns 15/4

Barbell bent over row   10/4 +5kg or 20/3

Keep your back straight on deadlifts. Add 2.5 kg to your bench press and deadlift, and 5 kg to your mid cable crossover and barbell bent over rows. If you can't perform most of the reps properly with increased weight, do as instructed and go heavier on your next workout. Rest 30 seconds between sets and 1 minute between exercises, except on bench press and deadlifts, where you should rest 1 minute between sets and 1 minute and 45 seconds between exercises.

Day 17 reps/sets

Abs

Sit ups   20/4

Hanging knee raises 15/4

Heel touches 10/4 (Each side)

Crunches   12/3

Keep your torso steady as possible on hanging knee raises. Rest 15 seconds between sets and 25 seconds between exercises.

Day 18 reps/sets

Yoga/ Stretching day

Use this day to recover from your workouts. Do 15-30 minutes of yoga or warm up and stretch all of the muscles which you have trained, including triceps, chest, abs, biceps, traps, lats, calves, quadriceps, hamstrings, glutes, delts, and your wrist flexors to boost out recovery.

Day 19 reps/sets

Biceps triceps and forearms

Barbell curls   10/5 +2.5kg, or 15/5

Hammer curls 10/4 with heavier dbs., or 15/4 (Each arm)

Lying cable curls   15/4

Skull crushers   12/4

Bodyweight dips   10/5

Barbell reverse curls   15/4

Add 2.5 kg to barbell curls, and switch to heavier dbs. on hammer curls. If you can't perform most of the reps with proper form, do as instructed and increase the weight on your next workout. Keep your upper arms stationary on all exercises, only your forearms should be moving, except on dips. Rest 25 seconds between sets and 35 seconds between exercises.

Day 20 reps/sets

Traps and shoulders

Military press   5/3 +2.5kg or 10/2

Dumbbell front raises 10/4
with heavier   dbs., or 15/6

Dumbbell lateral raises 10/4
with heavier dbs., or 15/6

Dumbbell bent over lateral raises 10/4
with heavier dbs.,   or 15/6

Barbell shrugs   10/6 +5kg or 20/3

Dumbbell shrugs 15/5

Add 2.5kg to your military press, 5 kg to your barbell shrugs, and switch to heavier kg on front, lateral and bent over raises. If you can't perform most of the reps with proper form, do as instructed and go heavier on your next workout. Rest 30 seconds between sets and 45 seconds between exercises, except on military press, where you should rest 45 seconds between sets and 1 minute and 30 seconds between exercises.

Day 21 reps/sets

Legs

Back Squat   5/3 +2.5kg or 10/2

Leg extension   10/5

Romanian deadlift 10/5

Seated calf raise   12/6 +5 kg or 30/4

Add +2.5 kg to your back squat, and 5 kg to your seated calf raise. If you can't perform most of the reps properly with increased weight, do as instructed and increase the weight on your next workout. Keep your back straight on back squats and romanian deadlifts. Rest 30 seconds between sets and 1 minute between exercises, except on back squats, where you should rest 1 minute between sets and 1 minute and 45 seconds between exercises.

Day 22 reps/sets

Chest and back

Bench press   5/3 +2.5kg or 10/2

DB bench press   10/5 with heavier
                  dbs. or 15/5

Mid Cable crossovers 12/7

Deadlift   5/3 +2.5kg or 10/2

Straight arm pulldowns 20/4

Barbell bent over row 15/4

Keep your back straight on deadlifts. Add 2.5 kg to your bench press and deadlift, and switch to heavier kg on bench press. If you can't perform most of the reps properly with increased weight, do as instructed and go heavier on your next workout. Rest 35 seconds between sets and 1 minute between exercises, except on bench press and deadlifts, where you should rest 1 minute between sets and 1 minute and 45 seconds between exercises.

Day 23 reps/sets

Abs

Sit ups   25/3

Hanging knee raises 20/3

Heel touches   12/3 (Each side)

Crunches   15/3

Keep your torso steady as possible on hanging knee raises. Rest 20 seconds between sets and 25 seconds between exercises.

Day 24 reps/sets

Rest day

Use this day to recover from your workouts. This doesn't mean that you should lie on the couch whole day without doing anything. Stretch all of the muscles which you have trained, including triceps, chest, abs, biceps, traps, lats, calves, quadriceps, hamstrings, glutes, delts, and your wrist flexors to boost out recovery.

Day 25 reps/sets

Biceps triceps and forearms

Skull crushers   15/4

Bodyweight dips   10/5

Barbell curls   12/5

Hammer curls 12/4   (Each arm)

Lying cable curls   10/4 +5kg or 20/3

Barbell reverse curls   10/4 2.5kg or 15/5

Add 2.5 kg to barbell reverse curls, and 5 kg to your lying cable curls. If you can't perform most of the reps with proper form, do as instructed and increase the weight on your next workout. Keep your upper arms stationary on all exercises , only your forearms should be moving, except on dips. Rest 25 seconds between sets and 35 seconds between exercises.

Day 26 reps/sets

Traps and shoulders

Military press   5/3 +2.5kg or 10/2

Barbell shrugs   10/6 +5kg or 20/3

Dumbbell shrugs   20/5

Dumbbell front raises   12/4

Dumbbell lateral raises   12/4

Dumbbell bent over lateral raises 12/4

Add 2.5kg to your military press and 5 kg to your barbell shrugs. If you can't perform most of the reps with proper form, do as instructed and go heavier on your next workout. Avoid swinging on front, lateral and bent over raises. Rest 30 seconds between sets and 45 seconds between exercises, except on military press, where you should rest 1 minute between sets and 1 minute and 45 seconds between exercises.

Day 27 reps/sets

Legs

Back Squat   5/3 +2.5kg or 10/2

Romanian deadlift 15/4

Leg extension   15/4

Seated calf raise   15/5

Add +2.5 kg to your back squat. If you can't perform most of the reps properly with increased weight, do as instructed and increase the weight on your next workout. Keep your back straight on back squats and romanian deadlifts. Rest 30 seconds between sets and 1 minute between exercises, except on back squats, where you should rest 1 minute between sets and 1 minute and 45 seconds between exercises.

Day 28 reps/sets

Chest and back

Bench press   5/3 +2.5kg or 10/2

Deadlift   5/3 +2.5kg or 10/2

DB bench press   12/4

Mid Cable crossovers 15/6

Pull ups   7/4

Barbell bent over row 15/5

Keep your back straight on deadlifts. Add 2.5 kg to your bench press and deadlift. If you can't perform most of the reps properly with increased weight, do as instructed and go heavier on your next workout. Rest 35 seconds between sets and 1 minute between exercises, except on bench press and deadlifts, where you should rest 1 minute between sets and 2 minutes between exercises.

Day 29 reps/sets

Abs

Sit ups   30/3

Hanging knee raises 20/4

Heel touches   15/3 (Each side)

Crunches   20/3

Keep your torso steady as possible on hanging knee raises. Rest 20 seconds between sets and 30 seconds between exercises.

Day 30 reps/sets

Rest day

Use this day to recover from your workouts.
This doesn't mean that you should lie on the
couch whole day without doing anything.
Stretch all of the muscles which you have
trained, including triceps, chest, abs, biceps,
traps, lats, calves, quadriceps, hamstrings,
glutes, delts, and your wrist flexors to boost
out recovery.

Day 31 reps/sets

Biceps triceps and forearms

Skull crushers   10/4 +2.5kg or 20/5

Bodyweight dips   15/5

Barbell curls   10/4 +2.5kg or 15/5

Hammer curls 12/4   (Each arm)

Lying cable curls   15/3

Barbell reverse curls   15/3

Add 2.5 kg to barbell curls, and skull crushers. If you can't perform most of the reps with proper form, do as instructed and increase the weight on your next workout. Keep your upper arms stationary on all exercises , only your forearms should be moving, except on dips. Rest 30 seconds between sets and 45 seconds between exercises.

Day 32 reps/sets

Traps and shoulders

Military press   5/3 +2.5kg or 10/2

Barbell shrugs   10/6 +5kg or 20/3

Dumbbell shrugs   25/4

Dumbbell front raises   12/5

Dumbbell lateral raises   12/5

Dumbbell bent over lateral raises 12/5

Add 2.5kg to your military press and 5 kg to your barbell shrugs. If you can't perform most of the reps with proper form, do as instructed and go heavier on your next workout. Avoid swinging on front, lateral and bent over raises. Rest 35 seconds between sets and 45 seconds between exercises, except on military press, where you should rest 1 minute between sets and 1 minute and 45 seconds between exercises.

Day 33 reps/sets

Legs

Back Squat   5/3 +2.5kg or 10/2

Romanian deadlift 15/5

Leg extension   15/5

Seated calf raise   20/4

Add +2.5 kg to your back squat. If you can't perform most of the reps properly with increased weight, do as instructed and increase the weight on your next workout. Keep your back straight on back squats and romanian deadlifts. Rest 30 seconds between sets and 1 minute between exercises, except on back squats, where you should rest 1 minute between sets and 1 minute and 45 seconds between exercises.

Day 34 reps/sets

Chest and back

Bench press   5/3 +2.5kg or 10/2

Deadlift   5/3 +2.5kg or 10/2

DB bench press   15/4

Mid Cable crossovers 20/5

Pull ups   8/4

Barbell bent over row 10/4 +5kg, or 20/4

Keep your back straight on deadlifts. Add 2.5 kg to your bench press and deadlift, and 5 kg to your barbell bent over row. If you can't perform most of the reps properly with increased weight, do as instructed and go heavier on your next workout. Rest 35 seconds between sets and 1 minute between exercises, except on bench press and deadlifts, where you should rest 1 minute between sets and 2 minutes between exercises.

Day 35 reps/sets

Abs

Sit ups   30/4

Hanging leg raises 10/4

Heel touches   15/4 (Each side)

Crunches   25/3

Keep your torso steady as possible on hanging leg raises. Rest 20 seconds between sets and 30 seconds between exercises.

Day 36 reps/sets

Rest day

Use this day to recover from your workouts.
This doesn't mean that you should lie on the
couch whole day without doing anything.
Stretch all of the muscles which you have
trained, including triceps, chest, abs, biceps,
traps, lats, calves, quadriceps, hamstrings,
glutes, delts, and your wrist flexors to boost
out recovery.

Day 37 reps/sets

Biceps triceps and forearms

Skull crushers   10/5

Bodyweight dips   20/5

Barbell curls   10/5

Hammer curls 15/4   (Each arm)

Lying cable curls   15/4

Barbell reverse curls   15/4

Keep your upper arms stationary on all exercises , only your forearms should be moving, except on dips. Rest 30 seconds between sets and 45 seconds between exercises.

Day 38 reps/sets

Traps and shoulders

Military press   5/3 +2.5kg or 10/2

Barbell shrugs   10/6 +5kg or 20/3

Dumbbell shrugs 10/4

with heavier dbs.   or 30/3

Dumbbell front raises   15/4

Dumbbell lateral raises   15/4

Dumbbell bent over lateral raises 15/4

Add 2.5kg to your military press and 5 kg to your barbell shrugs, and switch to heavier dumbbells on dumbbell shrugs. If you can't perform most of the reps with proper form, do as instructed and go heavier on your next workout. Avoid swinging on front, lateral and bent over raises. Rest 35 seconds between sets and 45 seconds between exercises, except on military press, where you should rest 1 minute between sets and 1 minute and 45 seconds between exercises.

Day 39 reps/sets

Legs

Back Squat   5/3 +2.5kg or 10/2

Romanian deadlift 10/4 +5kg or 20/5

Leg extension   10/4 +5kg or 20/5

Seated calf raise   25/4

Add +2.5 kg to your back squat, and 5kg to your romanian deadlift and leg extension. If you can't perform most of the reps properly with increased weight, do as instructed and increase the weight on your next workout. Keep your back straight on back squats and romanian deadlifts. Rest 30 seconds between sets and 1 minute between exercises, except on back squats, where you should rest 1 minute between sets and 1 minute and 45 seconds between exercises.

Day 40 reps/sets

Chest and back

Bench press   5/3 +2.5kg or 10/2

Deadlift   5/3 +2.5kg or 10/2

DB bench press   15/5

Mid Cable crossovers 10/6 +5kg or 20/6

Pull ups   10/4

Barbell bent over row   10/5

Keep your back straight on deadlifts. Add 2.5 kg to your bench press and deadlift, and 5 kg to your barbell bent over row. If you can't perform most of the reps properly with increased weight, do as instructed and go heavier on your next workout. Rest 35 seconds between sets and 1 minute between exercises, except on bench press and deadlifts, where you should rest 1 minute between sets and 2 minutes between exercises.

Day 41 reps/sets

Abs

Dragonflies   10/4

Hanging leg raises 10/5

Heel touches   20/3 (Each side)

Sit ups   15/4

Keep your torso steady as possible on hanging leg raises and dragonflies. Rest 20 seconds between sets and 30 seconds between exercises.

Day 42 reps/sets

Rest day

Use this day to recover from your workouts.
This doesn't mean that you should lie on the
couch whole day without doing anything.
Stretch all of the muscles which you have
trained, including triceps, chest, abs, biceps,
traps, lats, calves, quadriceps, hamstrings,
glutes, delts, and your wrist flexors to boost
out recovery.

Day 43 reps/sets

Biceps triceps and forearms

Barbell curls   15/4

Hammer curls 15/4   (Each arm)

Lying cable curls   10/4 +5kg or 20/3

Skull crushers   10/4 +2.5kg or 20/3

Weighted dips +5kg 10/5

Barbell reverse curls 10/4 +2.5kg or 20/3

Add 5 kg to your lying cable curls, and 2.5 kg to your barbell reverse curls and skull crushers. On weighted dips, fasten a dip belt, or alternatively a lifting belt around your waist , and attach a chain to it. Grasp a 5kg plate and attach it to the chain Keep your upper arms stationary on all exercises , only your forearms should be moving, except on dips. Rest 30 seconds between sets and 45 seconds between exercises.

Day 44   reps/sets

Traps and shoulders

Military press   5/3 +2.5kg or 10/2

Dumbbell front raises 10/4
with heavier dbs. or 15/5

Dumbbell lateral raises 10/4
with heavier dbs. or   15/5

Dumbbell bent over lateral raises 10/4
with   heavier dbs. or 15/5

Barbell shrugs   10/6 +5kg or 20/3
Dumbbell shrugs 10/5

Add 2.5kg to your military press and 5 kg to your barbell shrugs, and switch to heavier dumbbells on front, lateral, and bent over raises. If you can't perform most of the reps with a proper form, do as instructed and go heavier on your next workout. Rest 35 seconds between sets and 45 seconds between exercises, except on military press, where you should rest 1 minute between sets and 1 minute and 45 seconds between exercises.

Day 45 reps/sets

Legs

Back Squat   5/3 +2.5kg or 10/2

Romanian deadlift 12/4

Leg extension   10/5

Seated calf raise   15/4 +5kg, or 30/4

Add +2.5 kg to your back squat, and 5kg to your seated calf raise. If you can't perform most of the reps properly with increased weight, do as instructed and increase the weight on your next workout. Keep your back straight on back squats and romanian deadlifts. Rest 30 seconds between sets and 1 minute between exercises, except on back squats, where you should rest 1 minute between sets and 1 minute and 45 seconds between exercises.

Day 46 reps/sets

Chest and back

Bench press   5/3 +2.5kg or 10/2

DB bench press   10/5
with heavier dbs., or 20/5

Mid Cable crossovers 15/5

Deadlift   5/3 +2.5kg or 10/2

Pull ups   10/5

Barbell bent over row   12/5

Keep your back straight on deadlifts. Add 2.5 kg to your bench press and deadlift, and switch to heavier dumbbells on dumbbell bench press. If you can't perform most of the reps properly with increased weight, do as instructed and go heavier on your next workout. Rest 35 seconds between sets and 1 minute between exercises, except on bench press and deadlifts, where you should rest 1 minute between sets and 2 minutes between exercises.

Day 47 reps/sets

Abs

Dragonflies   12/4

Hanging leg raises 15/4

Hanging windshield wipers 10/4
(Each side)

Sit ups   15/4

Keep your torso steady as possible on
hanging leg raises, hanging windshield wipers,
and dragonflies. Rest 20 seconds between
sets and 35 seconds between exercises.

Day 48 reps/sets

Rest day

Use this day to recover from your workouts. This doesn't mean that you should lie on the couch whole day without doing nothing. Stretch all of the muscles which you have trained, including triceps, chest, abs, biceps, traps, lats, calves, quadriceps, hamstrings, glutes, delts, and your wrist flexors to boost out recovery.

Day 49 reps/sets
Biceps triceps and forearms

Barbell curls   15/5

Hammer curls   10/4...
with heavier dbs., or 15/5(Each arm)

Lying cable curls   12/5

Skull crushers   12/4

Weighted dips with 7.5kg 10/5,
or 15/5 with 5kg

Barbell reverse curls 10/5

Switch to heavier dbs. on hammer curls, or do as instructed and go heavier on your next workout. On weighted dips, fasten a dip belt, or alternatively a lifting belt around your waist, and attach a chain to it. Grasp a 5kg plate and 2.5kg plate, and attach them to the chain. If you can't perform reps properly with 7.5kg, do as instructed and go heavier on your next workout.. Rest 30 seconds between sets and 45 seconds between exercises.

Day 50 reps/sets

Traps and shoulders

Military press   5/3 +2.5kg or 10/2
Dumbbell front raises 12/4

Dumbbell lateral raises 12/4

Dumbbell bentover lateral raises 12/4

Barbell shrugs   10/6 +5kg or 20/3

Dumbbell shrugs 15/4

Add 2.5kg to your military press and 5 kg to your barbell shrugs. If you can't perform most of the reps with a proper form, do as instructed and go heavier on your next workout. Rest 35 seconds between sets and 45 seconds between exercises, except on military press, where you should rest 1 minute between sets and 1 minute and 45 seconds between exercises.

Day 51 reps/sets

Legs

Back Squat   5/3 +2.5kg or 10/2

Romanian deadlift 15/4

Leg extension   15/4

Seated calf raise   20/4

Add +2.5 kg to your back squat. If you can't perform most of the reps properly with increased weight, do as instructed and increase the weight on your next workout. Keep your back straight on back squats and romanian deadlifts. Rest 30 seconds between sets and 1 minute between exercises, except on back squats, where you should rest 1 minute between sets and 1 minute and 45 seconds between exercises.

Day 52 reps/sets

Chest and back

Bench press   5/3 +2.5kg or 10/2

DB bench press   10/5

Mid Cable crossovers 20/5

Deadlift   5/3 +2.5kg or 10/2

Pull ups   12/4

Barbell bent over row 15/5

Keep your back straight on deadlifts. Add 2.5 kg to your bench press and deadlift. If you can't perform most of the reps properly with increased weight, do as instructed and go heavier on your next workout. Rest 35 seconds between sets and 1 minute between exercises, except on bench press and deadlifts, where you should rest 1 minute between sets and 2 minutes between exercises.

Day 53 reps/sets

Abs

Dragonflies   15/4

Hanging leg raises 20/3

Hanging windshield wipers 12/4
(Each side)

Sit ups   20/3
Keep your torso steady as possible on
hanging leg raises, hanging windshield wipers,
and dragonflies. Rest 25 seconds between
sets and 35 seconds between exercises.

Day 54 reps/sets

Rest day

Use this day to recover from your workouts. This doesn't mean that you should lie on the couch whole day without doing anything. Stretch all of the muscles which you have trained, including triceps, chest, abs, biceps, traps, lats, calves, quadriceps, hamstrings, glutes, delts, and your wrist flexors to boost out recovery.

Day 55 reps/sets

Biceps triceps and forearms

Barbell curls   10/4 +2.5kg, or 15/5

Hammer curls   10/4 (Each arm)

Lying cable curls   15/5

Skull crushers   15/4

Weighted dips with 10 kg 10/5,
or 15/5 with 7.5 kg

Barbell reverse curls 12/4

On weighted dips, fasten a dip belt, or alternatively a lifting belt around your waist, and attach a chain to it. Grasp a 10kg plate, and attach it to the chain. If you can't perform reps properly with10 kg , do as instructed and go heavier on your next workout. Keep your upper arms stationary on all exercises, except on dips. Rest 30 seconds between sets and 45 seconds between exercises.

Day 56 reps/sets

Traps and shoulders

Military press   5/3 +2.5kg or 10/2
Dumbbell front raises 15/4

Dumbbell lateral raises 15/4

Dumbbell bent over lateral raises 15/4

Barbell shrugs   10/6 +5kg or 20/3

Dumbbell shrugs 20/4

Add 2.5kg to your military press and 5 kg to your barbell shrugs. If you can't perform most of the reps with a proper form, do as instructed and go heavier on your next workout. Rest 40 seconds between sets and 50 seconds between exercises, except on military press, where you should rest 1 minute between sets and 1 minute and 45 seconds between exercises.

Day 57 reps/sets

Legs

Back Squat   5/3 +2.5kg or 10/2

Romanian deadlift 10/4 +5kg or 15/5

Leg extension   10/4 +5kg or 15/5

Seated calf raise   30/3

Add +2.5 kg to your back squat, and 5kg to your romanian deadlift and leg extension. If you can't perform most of the reps properly with increased weight, do as instructed and increase the weight on your next workout. Keep your back straight on back squats and romanian deadlifts. Rest 30 seconds between sets and 1 minute between exercises, except on back squats, where you should rest 1 minute between sets and 1 minute and 45 seconds between exercises.

Day 58 reps/sets

Chest and back

Bench press   5/3 +2.5kg or 10/2

DB bench press   10/5

Mid Cable crossovers 10/6 +5kg or 20/6

Deadlift   5/3 +2.5kg or 10/2

Pull ups   12/5

Barbell bent over row   10/4 +5kg or 20/4

Keep your back straight on deadlifts. Add 2.5 kg to your bench press and deadlift, and 5kg to your mid cable cross over and bent over row. If you can't perform most of the reps properly with increased weight, do as instructed and go heavier on your next workout. Rest 35 seconds between sets and 1 minute between exercises, except on bench press and deadlifts, where you should rest 1 minute between sets and 2 minutes between exercises.

Day 59 reps/sets

Abs

Dragonflies   20/3

Hanging leg raises 20/4

Hanging windshield wipers 15/4
(Each side)

Sit ups   20/4

Keep your torso steady as possible on
hanging leg raises, hanging windshield wipers,
and dragonflies. Rest 25 seconds between
sets and 35 seconds between exercises.

Day 60 reps/sets

Rest day

Use this day to recover from your workouts. This doesn't mean that you should lie on the couch whole day without doing anything. Stretch all of the muscles which you have trained, including triceps, chest, abs, biceps, traps, lats, calves, quadriceps, hamstrings, glutes, delts, and your wrist flexors to boost out recovery.

Day 61 reps/sets

Biceps triceps and forearms

Barbell curls   15/5

Hammer curls   15/4 (Each arm)

Lying cable curls   20/4

Skull crushers   20/4

Bench dips   30/4

Dumbbell reverse curls 20/4 (Each arm)

Keep your upper arms stationary on all exercises , only your forearms should be moving, except on bench dips. Rest 20 seconds between sets and 35 seconds between exercises.

Day 62 reps/sets

Traps and shoulders

Military press   5/3 +2.5kg or 10/2

Dumbbell front raises 15/5

Dumbbell lateral raises 15/5

Dumbbell bent over lateral raises 15/5

Barbell shrugs   10/6 +5kg or 20/3

Dumbbell shrugs   25/3

Add 2.5kg to your military press, and 5 kg to your barbell shrugs. If you can't perform most of the reps with proper form, do as instructed and go heavier on your next workout. Avoid swinging on front, lateral and bent over raises. Rest 25 seconds between sets and 45 seconds between exercises, except on military press, where you should rest 45 seconds between sets and 1 minute and 30 seconds between exercises.

Day 63 reps/sets

Legs

Back Squat   5/3 +2.5kg or 10/2

Leg extension   15/5

Romanian deadlift 20/3

Seated calf raise   20/5

Add +2.5 kg to your back squat. If you can't perform 5 reps with increased weight, do as instructed and increase the weight on your next workout. Keep your back straight on back squats and romanian deadlifts. Rest 35 seconds between sets and 1 minute between exercises, except on back squats, where you should rest 1 minute between sets and 1 minute and 45 seconds between exercises.

Day 64 reps/sets

Chest and back

Bench press   5/3 +2.5kg or 10/2

DB bench press 15/5

Mid Cable crossovers 20/6

Deadlift   5/3 +2.5kg or 10/2

Straight arm pulldowns 10/5 +5kg or 20/3

Barbell bent over row   20/4

Keep your back straight on deadlifts. Add 2.5 kg to your bench press and deadlift, and 5 kg to your straight arm pulldown. If you can't perform most of the reps properly with increased weight, do as instructed and go heavier on your next workout. Rest 30 seconds between sets and 1 minute between exercises, except on bench press and deadlifts, where you should rest 1 minute between sets and 1 minute and 45 seconds between exercises.

Day 65 reps/sets

Abs

Sit ups	25/5
Hanging knee raises	15/5
Crunches	25/5

Keep your torso steady as possible on hanging knee raises. Rest 10 seconds between sets and 20 seconds between exercises.

Day 66 reps/sets

Rest day

Use this day to recover from your workouts. This doesn't mean that you should lie on the couch whole day without doing anything. Stretch all of the muscles which you have trained, including triceps, chest, abs, biceps, traps, lats, calves, quadriceps, hamstrings, glutes, delts, and your wrist flexors to boost out recovery.

Day 67 reps/sets

Biceps triceps and forearms

Barbell curls	15/5
Hammer curls	12/4 (Each arm)
Lying cable curls	12/4 +5kg, or 20/3
Skull crushers	12/4 +2.5 kg or 20/3
Bodyweight dips	15/5
Barbell reverse curls	10/5 +2.5kg or 20/3 (Each arm)

Add 2.5 kg to your skull crushers and barbell reverse curls, and 5 kg to your lying cable curls. If you can't perform most of the reps with proper form, do as instructed and increase the weight on your next workout. Keep your upper arms stationary on all exercises, only your forearms should be moving, except on dips. Rest 25 seconds between sets and 35 seconds between exercises.

Day 68 reps/sets

Traps and shoulders

Military press   5/3 +2.5kg or 10/2

Dumbbell front raises 15/6

Dumbbell lateral raises 15/6

Dumbbell bent over lateral raises 15/6

Barbell shrugs   10/6 +5kg or 20/4

Dumbbell shrugs 10/5 with heavier dbs.
          or   20/5

Add 2.5kg to your military press, 5 kg to your barbell shrugs, and switch to heavier dbs. on dumbbell shrugs. If you can't perform most of the reps with proper form, do as instructed and go heavier on your next workout. Avoid swinging on front, lateral and bent over raises. Rest 30 seconds between sets and 45 seconds between exercises, except on military press, where you should rest 45 seconds between sets and 1 minute and 30 seconds between exercises.

Day 69 reps/sets

Legs

Back Squat   5/3 +2.5kg or 10/2

Leg extension   10/4 +5kg or 20/3

Romanian deadlift 10/4 +5kg or 20/3

Seated calf raise   25/4

Add +2.5 kg to your back squat, and 5 kg to your leg extension and romanian deadlift. If you can't perform most of the reps properly with increased weight, do as instructed and increase the weight on your next workout. Keep your back straight on back squats and romanian deadlifts. Rest 35 seconds between sets and 1 minute between exercises, except on back squats, where you should rest 1 minute between sets and 1 minute and 45 seconds between exercises.

Day 70 reps/sets

Chest and back

Bench press   5/3 +2.5kg or 10/2

DB bench press 12/5

Mid Cable crossovers 10/6 +5kg or 20/4

Deadlift   5/3 +2.5kg or 10/2

Straight arm pulldowns 15/4

Barbell bent over row   10/4 +5kg or 20/3

Keep your back straight on deadlifts. Add 2.5 kg to your bench press and deadlift, and 5 kg to your mid cable crossover and barbell bent over rows. If you can't perform most of the reps properly with increased weight, do as instructed and go heavier on your next workout. Rest 30 seconds between sets and 1 minute between exercises, except on bench press and deadlifts, where you should rest 1 minute between sets and 1 minute and 45 seconds between exercises.

Day 71 reps/sets

Abs

Sit ups 30/4

Hanging knee raises 15/6

Heel touches 20/4 (Each side)

Crunches 30/3

Keep your torso steady as possible on hanging knee raises. Rest 15 seconds between sets and 25 seconds between exercises.

Day 72 reps/sets

Yoga/ Stretching day

Use this day to recover from your workouts. Do 15-30 minutes of yoga or warm up and stretch all of the muscles which you have trained, including triceps, chest, abs, biceps, traps, lats, calves, quadriceps, hamstrings, glutes, delts, and your wrist flexors to boost out recovery.

Day 73 reps/sets

Biceps triceps and forearms

Skull crushers   10/4 +2.5kg or 20/5

Bodyweight dips   20/5

Barbell curls   10/4 +2.5kg or 15/5

Hammer curls 20/4   (Each arm)

Lying cable curls   20/3

Barbell reverse curls   20/3

Add 2.5 kg to barbell curls, and skull crushers. If you can't perform most of the reps with proper form, do as instructed and increase the weight on your next workout. Keep your upper arms stationary on all exercises , only your forearms should be moving, except on dips. Rest 30 seconds between sets and 45 seconds between exercises.

Day 74 reps/sets

Traps and shoulders

Military press	5/3 +2.5kg or 10/4
Barbell shrugs	10/6 +5kg or 20/4
Dumbbell shrugs	25/6
Dumbbell front raises	12/6
Dumbbell lateral raises	12/6
Dumbbell bent over lateral raises	12/6

Add 2.5kg to your military press and 5 kg to your barbell shrugs. If you can't perform most of the reps with proper form, do as instructed and go heavier on your next workout. Avoid swinging on front, lateral and bent over raises. Rest 35 seconds between sets and 45 seconds between exercises, except on military press, where you should rest 1 minute between sets and 1 minute and 45 seconds between exercises.

Day 75 reps/sets

Legs

Back Squat   5/3 +2.5kg or 10/2

Romanian deadlift 20/5

Leg extension   20/5

Seated calf raise   25/4

Add +2.5 kg to your back squat. If you can't perform most of the reps properly with increased weight, do as instructed and increase the weight on your next workout. Keep your back straight on back squats and romanian deadlifts. Rest 30 seconds between sets and 1 minute between exercises, except on back squats, where you should rest 1 minute between sets and 1 minute and 45 seconds between exercises.

Day 76 reps/sets

Chest and back

Bench press   5/3 +2.5kg or 10/2

Deadlift   5/3 +2.5kg or 10/2

DB bench press   15/4

Mid Cable crossovers 20/5

Pull ups   10/4

Barbell bent over row 10/4 +5kg, or 20/4

Keep your back straight on deadlifts. Add 2.5 kg to your bench press and deadlift, and 5 kg to your barbell bent over row. If you can't perform most of the reps properly with increased weight, do as instructed and go heavier on your next workout. Rest 35 seconds between sets and 1 minute between exercises, except on bench press and deadlifts, where you should rest 1 minute between sets and 2 minutes between exercises.

Day 77 reps/sets

Abs

Sit ups   40/4

Hanging leg raises 15/4

Heel touches   15/5 (Each side)

Crunches   25/5

Keep your torso steady as possible on hanging leg raises. Rest 20 seconds between sets and 30 seconds between exercises.

Day 78 reps/sets

Rest day

Use this day to recover from your workouts.
This doesn't mean that you should lie on the
couch whole day without doing anything.
Stretch all of the muscles which you have
trained, including triceps, chest, abs, biceps,
traps, lats, calves, quadriceps, hamstrings,
glutes, delts, and your wrist flexors to boost
out recovery.

Day 79 reps/sets

Biceps triceps and forearms

Skull crushers   10/5

Bodyweight dips   20/5

Barbell curls   10/5

Hammer curls 15/4   (Each arm)

Lying cable curls   15/4

Barbell reverse curls   15/4

Keep your upper arms stationary on all exercises , only your forearms should be moving, except on dips. Rest 30 seconds between sets and 45 seconds between exercises.

Day 80 reps/sets

Traps and shoulders

Military press   5/3 +2.5kg or 10/2

Barbell shrugs   10/6 +5kg or 20/3

Dumbbell shrugs 10/4

with heavier dbs.   or 30/3

Dumbbell front raises   15/4

Dumbbell lateral raises   15/4

Dumbbell bent over lateral raises 15/4

Add 2.5kg to your military press and 5 kg to your barbell shrugs, and switch to heavier dumbbells on dumbbell shrugs. If you can't perform most of the reps with proper form, do as instructed and go heavier on your next workout. Avoid swinging on front, lateral and bent over raises. Rest 35 seconds between sets and 45 seconds between exercises, except on military press, where you should rest 1 minute between sets and 1 minute and 45 seconds between exercises.

Day 81 reps/sets

Legs

Back Squat   5/3 +2.5kg or 10/2

Romanian deadlift 10/4 +5kg or 20/5

Leg extension   10/4 +5kg or 20/5

Seated calf raise   25/4

Add +2.5 kg to your back squat, and 5kg to your romanian deadlift and leg extension. If you can't perform most of the reps properly with increased weight, do as instructed and increase the weight on your next workout. Keep your back straight on back squats and romanian deadlifts. Rest 30 seconds between sets and 1 minute between exercises, except on back squats, where you should rest 1 minute between sets and 1 minute and 45 seconds between exercises.

Day 82 reps/sets

Chest and back

Bench press   5/3 +2.5kg or 10/2

Deadlift   5/3 +2.5kg or 10/2

DB bench press   15/5

Mid Cable crossovers 10/6 +5kg or 20/6

Pull ups   10/4

Barbell bent over row 10/5

Keep your back straight on deadlifts. Add 2.5 kg to your bench press and deadlift, and 5 kg to your barbell bent over row. If you can't perform most of the reps properly with increased weight, do as instructed and go heavier on your next workout. Rest 35 seconds between sets and 1 minute between exercises, except on bench press and deadlifts, where you should rest 1 minute between sets and 2 minutes between exercises.

Day 83 reps/sets

Abs

Dragonflies   15/4

Hanging leg raises 20/5

Heel touches   20/5 (Each side)

Sit ups   30/4

Keep your torso steady as possible on hanging leg raises and dragonflies. Rest 20 seconds between sets and 30 seconds between exercises.

Day 84 reps/sets

Rest day

Use this day to recover from your workouts. This doesn't mean that you should lie on the couch whole day without doing anything. Stretch all of the muscles which you have trained, including triceps, chest, abs, biceps, traps, lats, calves, quadriceps, hamstrings, glutes, delts, and your wrist flexors to boost out recovery.

Day 85 reps/sets
Biceps triceps and forearms

Barbell curls   15/5

Hammer curls   10/4...
with heavier dbs., or 15/5(Each arm)

Lying cable curls   12/5

Skull crushers   12/4

Weighted dips with 7.5kg 10/5,
or 15/5 with 5kg

Barbell reverse curls 10/5

Switch to heavier dbs. on hammer curls, or do as instructed and go heavier on your next workout. On weighted dips, fasten a dip belt, or alternatively a lifting belt around your waist, and attach a chain to it. Grasp a 5kg plate and 2.5kg plate, and attach them to the chain. If you can't perform reps properly with 7.5kg, do as instructed and go heavier on your next workout.. Rest 30 seconds between sets and 45 seconds between exercises.

Day 86 reps/sets

Traps and shoulders

Military press   5/3 +2.5kg or 10/2
Dumbbell front raises 12/4

Dumbbell lateral raises 12/4

Dumbbell bentover lateral raises 12/4

Barbell shrugs   10/6 +5kg or 20/3

Dumbbell shrugs 15/4

Add 2.5kg to your military press and 5 kg to your barbell shrugs. If you can't perform most of the reps with a proper form, do as instructed and go heavier on your next workout. Rest 35 seconds between sets and 45 seconds between exercises, except on military press, where you should rest 1 minute between sets and 1 minute and 45 seconds between exercises.

Day 87 reps/sets

Legs

Back Squat   5/3 +2.5kg or 10/2

Romanian deadlift 15/4

Leg extension   15/4

Seated calf raise   20/4

Add +2.5 kg to your back squat. If you can't perform most of the reps properly with increased weight, do as instructed and increase the weight on your next workout. Keep your back straight on back squats and romanian deadlifts. Rest 30 seconds between sets and 1 minute between exercises, except on back squats, where you should rest 1 minute between sets and 1 minute and 45 seconds between exercises.

Day 88 reps/sets

Chest and back

Bench press   5/3 +2.5kg or 10/2

DB bench press   10/5

Mid Cable crossovers 20/5

Deadlift   5/3 +2.5kg or 10/2

Pull ups   12/4

Barbell bent over row 15/5

Keep your back straight on deadlifts. Add 2.5 kg to your bench press and deadlift. If you can't perform most of the reps properly with increased weight, do as instructed and go heavier on your next workout. Rest 35 seconds between sets and 1 minute between exercises, except on bench press and deadlifts, where you should rest 1 minute between sets and 2 minutes between exercises.

Day 89 reps/sets

Abs

Dragonflies   25/4

Hanging leg raises 20/5

Hanging windshield wipers 15/4
(Each side)

Sit ups   20/6
Keep your torso steady as possible on
hanging leg raises, hanging windshield wipers,
and dragonflies. Rest 25 seconds between
sets and 35 seconds between exercises.

Day 90 reps/sets

Rest day

Use this day to recover from your workouts. This doesn't mean that you should lie on the couch whole day without doing anything. Stretch all of the muscles which you have trained, including triceps, chest, abs, biceps, traps, lats, calves, quadriceps, hamstrings, glutes, delts, and your wrist flexors to boost out recovery.

Day 91 reps/sets

Biceps triceps and forearms

Skull crushers   10/5

Bodyweight dips   20/5

Barbell curls   10/5

Hammer curls 15/4   (Each arm)

Lying cable curls   15/4

Barbell reverse curls   15/4

Keep your upper arms stationary on all exercises , only your forearms should be moving, except on dips. Rest 30 seconds between sets and 45 seconds between exercises.

Day 92 reps/sets

Traps and shoulders

Military press   5/3 +2.5kg or 10/2

Barbell shrugs   10/6 +5kg or 20/3

Dumbbell shrugs 10/4

with heavier dbs.   or 30/3

Dumbbell front raises   15/4

Dumbbell lateral raises   15/4

Dumbbell bent over lateral raises 15/4

Add 2.5kg to your military press and 5 kg to your barbell shrugs, and switch to heavier dumbbells on dumbbell shrugs. If you can't perform most of the reps with proper form, do as instructed and go heavier on your next workout. Avoid swinging on front, lateral and bent over raises. Rest 35 seconds between sets and 45 seconds between exercises, except on military press, where you should rest 1 minute between sets and 1 minute and 45 seconds between exercises.

Day 93 reps/sets

Legs

Back Squat   5/3 +2.5kg or 10/2

Romanian deadlift 10/4 +5kg or 20/5

Leg extension   10/4 +5kg or 20/5

Seated calf raise   25/4

Add +2.5 kg to your back squat, and 5kg to your romanian deadlift and leg extension. If you can't perform most of the reps properly with increased weight, do as instructed and increase the weight on your next workout. Keep your back straight on back squats and romanian deadlifts. Rest 30 seconds between sets and 1 minute between exercises, except on back squats, where you should rest 1 minute between sets and 1 minute and 45 seconds between exercises.

Day 94 reps/sets

Chest and back

Bench press   5/3 +2.5kg or 10/2

Deadlift   5/3 +2.5kg or 10/2

DB bench press   15/5

Mid Cable crossovers 10/6 +5kg or 20/6

Pull ups   10/4

Barbell bent over row 10/5

Keep your back straight on deadlifts. Add 2.5 kg to your bench press and deadlift, and 5 kg to your barbell bent over row. If you can't perform most of the reps properly with increased weight, do as instructed and go heavier on your next workout. Rest 35 seconds between sets and 1 minute between exercises, except on bench press and deadlifts, where you should rest 1 minute between sets and 2 minutes between exercises.

Day 95 reps/sets

Abs

Dragonflies   10/4

Hanging leg raises 10/5

Heel touches   20/3 (Each side)

Sit ups   15/4

Keep your torso steady as possible on hanging leg raises and dragonflies. Rest 20 seconds between sets and 30 seconds between exercises.

Day 96 reps/sets

Rest day

Use this day to recover from your workouts. This doesn't mean that you should lie on the couch whole day without doing anything. Stretch all of the muscles which you have trained, including triceps, chest, abs, biceps, traps, lats, calves, quadriceps, hamstrings, glutes, delts, and your wrist flexors to boost out recovery.

Day 97 reps/sets

Biceps triceps and forearms

Barbell curls   15/4

Hammer curls   15/4   (Each arm)

Lying cable curls   10/4 +5kg or 20/3

Skull crushers   10/4 +2.5kg or 20/3

Weighted dips +5kg   10/5

Barbell reverse curls   10/4 +2.5kg or 20/3

Add 5 kg to your lying cable curls, and 2.5 kg to your barbell reverse curls and skull crushers. On weighted dips, fasten a dip belt, or alternatively a lifting belt around your waist , and attach a chain to it. Grasp a 5kg plate and attach it to the chain Keep your upper arms stationary on all exercises , only your forearms should be moving, except on dips. Rest 30 seconds between sets and 45 seconds between exercises.

Day 98 reps/sets

Traps and shoulders

Military press   5/3 +2.5kg or 10/2

Dumbbell front raises 10/4
with heavier dbs. or 15/5

Dumbbell lateral raises 10/4
with heavier dbs. or   15/5

Dumbbell bent over lateral raises 10/4
with   heavier dbs. or 15/5

Barbell shrugs   10/6 +5kg or 20/3
Dumbbell shrugs 10/5

Add 2.5kg to your military press and 5 kg to your barbell shrugs, and switch to heavier dumbbells on front, lateral, and bent over raises. If you can't perform most of the reps with a proper form, do as instructed and go heavier on your next workout. Rest 35 seconds between sets and 45 seconds between exercises, except on military press, where you should rest 1 minute between sets and 1 minute and 45 seconds between exercises.

Day 99 reps/sets

Legs

Back Squat   5/3 +2.5kg or 10/2

Romanian deadlift 12/4

Leg extension   10/5

Seated calf raise   15/4 +5kg, or 30/4

Add +2.5 kg to your back squat, and 5kg to your seated calf raise. If you can't perform most of the reps properly with increased weight, do as instructed and increase the weight on your next workout. Keep your back straight on back squats and romanian deadlifts. Rest 30 seconds between sets and 1 minute between exercises, except on back squats, where you should rest 1 minute between sets and 1 minute and 45 seconds between exercises.

Abs

Dragonflies   12/4

Hanging leg raises 15/4

Hanging windshield wipers 10/4
(Each side)

Sit ups   15/4

Keep your torso steady as possible on hanging leg raises, hanging windshield wipers, and dragonflies. Rest 20 seconds between sets and 35 seconds between exercises.

Day 100 reps/sets

Recovery day

It is time to admire your results. You have completed 100 days of intense training. Great job!

Chapter 2:
Strength from Within

"Because we are what we eat we can literally transform our bodies and minds." M. Adams

Feeding your body properly is crucial to performing at a top level. Your body runs on whatever you feed it. Your meals are your fuel. If you want your body to perform at its full potential, you must keep it perfectly fine tuned.

Each day you will find a right balance of protein, carbs, fiber and fat to keep your body at optimal levels. I would like to suggest you modify this plan according to your own weight, age, health condition and workouts as well. Choose your meals according to what time of day you will be training. For example, before a workout you would need more energy so you would choose a meal which would contain more carbohydrates. After a workout you would need to replenish your body so I would suggest either a snack or a meal with a greater amount of protein.

If a certain ingredient mentioned in a daily meal is not in season or not available near you, you may choose another healthy and nutritious alternative. The main goal is to fuel your body in the best way possible so it can help you achieve your dreams.

Day 1
Breakfast:
½ cup rolled oats
1 tbsp flaxseed
½ cup coconut milk
Nutritional values: Kcal: 468 Protein: 9.4g, Carbs: 36.4g, Dietary Fiber: 8.7g, Fats: 33.5g
Snack:
1 oz pecans
1 large orange
Nutritional values: Kcal: 284 Protein: 4.8g, Carbs: 25.7g, Dietary Fiber: 7.5g, Fats: 4.8g
Lunch:
1 large zucchini, grilled and seasoned with 1 tbsp olive oil
2 slices buckwheat bread
1 pear
Nutritional values: Kcal: 403 Protein: 8.7g, Carbs: 60.7g, Dietary Fiber: 9.2g, Fats: 16.6g
Snack:
3 cups pineapple chunks, juiced
1 large apple, juiced
Nutritional values: Kcal: 315 Protein: 3.5g, Carbs: 92g, Dietary Fiber: 12.7g, Fats: 0.9g
Dinner
10 oz mushrooms, grilled
½ cup basmati rice, cooked
Nutritional values: Kcal: 398 Protein: 15.5g, Carbs: 83.3g, Dietary Fiber: 4g, Fats: 1.4g

Day2

Breakfast:

1 cup almond yogurt

1 tbsp chia seeds

3 figs

1 cup of black coffee

Nutritional values: Kcal: 457 Protein: 22.1g, Carbs: 64.2g, Dietary Fiber: 16g, Fats: 13.1g

Snack:

½ avocado, grilled

3 plums

Nutritional values: Kcal: 295 Protein: 3.4g, Carbs: 32.6g, Dietary Fiber: 9.4g, Fats: 20.2g

Lunch:

1 cup green peas, cooked

½ cup hummus

7 oz mushrooms, grilled

1.5 oz cauliflower, grilled

Nutritional values: Kcal: 392 Protein: 25.9g, Carbs: 50.6g, Dietary Fiber: 19.4g, Fats: 13.2g

Snack:

1 large apple

2 medium-sized carrots

2 oz prunes

Nutritional values: Kcal: 302 Protein: 2.8g, Carbs: 79g, Dietary Fiber: 12.4g, Fats: 0.6g

Dinner:

7 oz buckwheat noodles, cooked and seasoned with one tablespoon of olive oil

2 oz spring onions, steamed

Nutritional values: Kcal: 412 Protein: 10.1g, Carbs: 54.1g, Dietary Fiber: 3.8g, Fats: 18.2g

Day 3
Breakfast:
10 oz tomatoes, grilled
7 oz asparagus, grilled
1 cup of freshly squeezed orange juice
4 large figs
Nutritional values: Kcal: 392 Protein: 11.1g,
Carbs: 93.1g, Dietary Fiber: 15.5g, Fats: 2g
Snack:
1 cup grapes
1 large mango
2 kiwis
Nutritional values: Kcal: 355 Protein: 5.1g, Carbs:
88.1g, Dietary Fiber: 10.4g, Fats: 2.4g
Lunch:
7 oz artichoke
½ cup kidney beans
1 tbsp extra virgin olive oil
Nutritional values: Kcal: 523 Protein: 27.2g,
Carbs: 77.2g, Dietary Fiber: 24.7g, Fats: 15.3g
Snack:
1 large apple
Nutritional values: Kcal: 116 Protein: 0.6g, Carbs:
30.8g, Dietary Fiber: 5.4g, Fats: 0.4g
Dinner:
7 oz arugula
1 cup raspberries
1 oz walnuts
1 cup freshly squeezed orange juice
Nutritional values: Kcal: 401 Protein: 15.1g,
Carbs: 50.5g, Dietary Fiber: 13.6g, Fats: 19.3g

Day 4
Breakfast:
2 bananas
1 tbsp pure coconut nectar
1 tbsp flaxseed
1 cup freshly squeezed lemonade
Nutritional values: Kcal: 369 Protein: 5.9g, Carbs: 78.3g, Dietary Fiber: 9.1g, Fats: 4.9g
Snack:
½ cup blueberries
1 oz almonds, toasted
1 oz walnuts
Nutritional values: Kcal: 381 Protein: 13.4g, Carbs: 19.4g, Dietary Fiber: 7.2g, Fats: 31.2g
Lunch:
3 oz red lentils, cooked
1 carrot cooked
7 oz kale, steamed
2 oz lettuce
Nutritional values: Kcal: 435 Protein: 28.7g, Carbs: 80.6g, Dietary Fiber: 31g, Fats: 1g
Snack:
3 cups honeydew melon, juiced
1 cup watermelon, diced
Nutritional values: Kcal: 203 Protein: 3.5g, Carbs: 55g, Dietary Fiber: 4.5g, Fats: 0.9g
Dinner:
5 oz eggplant, steamed
½ cup red lentils, cooked
2 cherry tomatoes, fresh
Nutritional values: Kcal: 419 Protein: 28.3g, Carbs: 75.6g, Dietary Fiber: 37.2g, Fats: 1.8g

Day 5:
Breakfast:
½ cup quinoa, cooked
3 tbsp raisins
¼ cup coconut milk
1 cup of black coffee
Nutritional values: Kcal: 532 Protein: 14.2g,
Carbs: 79.4g, Dietary Fiber: 8.3g, Fats: 19.6g
Snack:
1 oz pecan nuts
Nutritional values: Kcal: 197 Protein: 3g, Carbs:
4g, Dietary Fiber: 3g, Fats: 20.2g
Lunch:
2 medium-sized corn tortillas
¼ cup black beans, cooked
1 large tomato, diced
7 oz of spinach, steamed
1 red bell pepper
Nutritional values: Kcal: 386 Protein: 21.7g,
Carbs: 75g, Dietary Fiber: 18.5g, Fats: 3.5g
Snack:
1 cup cantaloupe
6 dates
Nutritional values: Kcal: 193 Protein: 2.5g, Carbs:
50.1g, Dietary Fiber: 5.4g, Fats: 0.5g
Dinner:
1 cup edamame hummus
½ cup beets, cooked
½ cup shallots, fresh
Nutritional values: Kcal: 471 Protein: 36.6g,
Carbs: 50.2g, Dietary Fiber: 12.4g, Fats: 17.6g

Day 6:

Breakfast:

1 cup of strawberries, fresh

½ cup raspberries, fresh

5 almonds, toasted

½ cup almond yogurt

1 cup of herbal tea

Nutritional values: Kcal: 200 Protein: 10g, Carbs: 28.3g, Dietary Fiber: 7.6g, Fats: 5.3g

Snack:

1 peach

2 oz pecan nuts

Nutritional values: Kcal: 454 Protein: 7.5g, Carbs: 22.1g, Dietary Fiber: 8.4g, Fats: 40.9g

Lunch:

4 Roma tomatoes, grilled

½ cup rice, cooked

½ spinach, steamed

Nutritional values: Kcal: 436 Protein: 11.9g, Carbs: 92g, Dietary Fiber: 9.5g, Fats: 3.6g

Snack:

1 red bell pepper

1 yellow bell pepper

1 green bell pepper

1 cup avocado chunks

Nutritional values: Kcal: 412 Protein: 6.4g, Carbs: 39.6g, Dietary Fiber: 14.6g, Fats: 29.4g

Dinner:

3.5 oz buckwheat pasta, cooked

1 large tomato

3.5 oz lettuce

Nutritional values: Kcal: 330 Protein: 13.2g, Carbs: 63.9g, Dietary Fiber: 2.7g, Fats: 2.8g

Day 7:
Breakfast:
2 large oranges, broiled
2 oz walnuts
1 cup of herbal tea
Nutritional values: Kcal: 523 Protein: 17.1g,
Carbs: 48.9g, Dietary Fiber: 12.7g, Fats: 33.9g
Snack:
4 medium-sized oranges, juiced
Nutritional values: Kcal: 200 Protein: 4.9g, Carbs:
64.5g, Dietary Fiber: 12.4g, Fats: 0.6g
Lunch:
2 cup butternut squash, cooked
1 cup Brussel sprouts, cooked
1 cup leeks, cooked
1 tbsp olive oil
Nutritional values: Kcal: 338 Protein: 71g, Carbs:
53.3g, Dietary Fiber: 10.5g, Fats: 14.8g
Snack:
7 oz chestnuts, baked
Nutritional values: Kcal: 389 Protein: 3.2g, Carbs:
87.7g, Dietary Fiber: 8.7g, Fats: 2.5g
Dinner:
5 oz orzo pasta, cooked
½ cup zucchini, grilled
Nutritional values: Kcal: 417 Protein: 16.7g,
Carbs: 79.5g, Dietary Fiber: 0.6g, Fats: 3.4g

Day 8:
Breakfast:

10 oz grilled red peppers

10 oz melon

4 pecans

1 cup of herbal tea

Nutritional values: Kcal: 212 Protein: 7.7g, Carbs: 48.6g, Dietary Fiber: 6.8g, Fats: 1.8g

Snack:

1 oz pecan nuts

Nutritional values: Kcal: 395 Protein: 6.1g, Carbs: 8.1g, Dietary Fiber: 6.1g, Fats: 40.5g

Lunch:

5 oz mushrooms, grilled

1 white onion, grilled

1 tbsp olive oil

Nutritional values: Kcal: 241 Protein: 3.4g, Carbs: 29.8g, Dietary Fiber: 5.3g, Fats: 14.4g

Snack:

7 oz avocado, baked

Nutritional values: Kcal: 405 Protein: 3.8g, Carbs: 17.1g, Dietary Fiber: 13.3g, Fats: 38.7g

Dinner:

1 tomato, fire-roasted

1 zucchini, grilled

7 oz turnip greens, fresh

1 oz walnuts

1 cup freshly squeezed orange juice

Nutritional values: Kcal: 393 Protein: 14.4g, Carbs: 51.7g, Dietary Fiber: 11.7g, Fats: 18.3g

Day 9:
Breakfast:
10 oz grilled red peppers
2 oz quinoa, cooked
10 oz melon
4 pecans
1 cup of herbal tea
Nutritional values: Kcal: 421 Protein: 15.7g,
Carbs: 85g, Dietary Fiber: 10.8g, Fats: 5.2g
Snack:
1 kiwi
1.5 oz almonds, toasted
Nutritional values: Kcal: 292 Protein: 9.9g, Carbs:
20.2g, Dietary Fiber: 7.6g, Fats: 21.7g
Lunch:
5 oz arugula, fresh
½ cup white beans, cooked
1 red onion, fresh
Nutritional values: Kcal: 416 Protein: 28.5g,
Carbs: 76.3g, Dietary Fiber: 20g, Fats: 1.9g
Snack:
1 medium apple
1 banana
Nutritional values: Kcal: 221 Protein: 1.9g, Carbs:
57.8g, Dietary Fiber: 8.5g, Fats: 0.8g
Dinner:
3.5 oz buckwheat noodles, cooked and seasoned
with one tablespoon of olive oil
2 oz spring onions, steamed
3.5 oz kale, steamed
Nutritional values: Kcal: 512 Protein: 16.1g,
Carbs: 83.1g, Dietary Fiber: 12.7g, Fats: 17.2g

Day 10
Breakfast:
¼ cup rolled oats
¼ cup almond milk
5 oz cherries
Nutritional values: Kcal: 379 Protein: 4.6g, Carbs: 56.8g, Dietary Fiber: 4.2g, Fats: 15.7g
Snack:
2 peaches
1 oz walnuts
Nutritional values: Kcal: 293 Protein: 9.6g, Carbs: 30.8g, Dietary Fiber: 6.5g, Fats: 17.5g
Lunch:
7 oz hummus
1 oz buckwheat bread
7 oz carrot sticks
Nutritional values: Kcal: 486 Protein: 19.5g, Carbs: 62.2g, Dietary Fiber: 17.5g, Fats: 20g
Snack:
3.5 oz cherries
Nutritional values: Kcal: 114 Protein: 0.4g, Carbs: 27.8g, Dietary Fiber: 0.6g, Fats: 0.1g
Dinner:
7 oz sweet potato, baked
¼ cup kidney beans, cooked
1 oz buckwheat bread
1 cup of herbal tea
Nutritional values: Kcal: 410 Protein: 16.5g, Carbs: 83.6g, Dietary Fiber: 14.3g, Fats: 1.8g

Day 11:

Breakfast

1 cup almond yogurt
7 oz pineapple chunks
1 large orange
1 cup of herbal tea
Nutritional values: Kcal: 362 Protein: 16.8g,
Carbs: 65.4g, Dietary Fiber: 7.2g, Fats: 3.5g

Snack:

2 slices buckwheat bread
1 medium-sized tomato, fresh
1 small cucumber
1 red onion, fresh
1 tbsp olive oil
Nutritional values: Kcal: 268 Protein: 5.1g, Carbs:
32.7g, Dietary Fiber: 5g, Fats: 15.1g

Lunch:

3.5 oz enoki mushrooms, grilled
7 oz shiitake mushrooms, grilled
3.5 oz shishito peppers, grilled
2 oz buckwheat bread
Nutritional values: Kcal: 550 Protein: 20.6g,
Carbs: 127g, Dietary Fiber: 34.3g, Fats: 5.8g

Snack:

7 oz cherries
Nutritional values: Kcal: 228 Protein: 0.7g, Carbs:
55.6g, Dietary Fiber: 1.2g, Fats: 0.1g

Dinner:

½ cup black beans, cooked
1 tbsp tahini
Nutritional values: Kcal: 420 Protein: 23.5g,
Carbs: 63.7g, Dietary Fiber: 16.1g, Fats: 9.4g

Day 12:
Breakfast:
1 cup almond yogurt
1 tbsp chia seeds
3 figs
1 cup of black coffee
Nutritional values: Kcal: 457 Protein: 22.1g,
Carbs: 64.2g, Dietary Fiber: 16g, Fats: 13.1g
Snack:
½ cup leek, cooked
1 medium-sized potato, cooked
½ cup shallots, cooked
1 tbsp olive oil
Nutritional values: Kcal: 369 Protein: 7g, Carbs:
56.9g, Dietary Fiber: 5.5g, Fats: 14.4g
Lunch:
1 cup edamame hummus
½ cup beets, cooked
½ cup shallots, fresh
Nutritional values: Kcal: 471 Protein: 36.6g,
Carbs: 50.2g, Dietary Fiber: 12.4g, Fats: 17.6g
Snack:
1 cup of freshly squeezed lemon juice
1.5 oz walnuts
Nutritional values: Kcal: 321 Protein: 12.2g,
Carbs: 9.3g, Dietary Fiber: 3.9g, Fats: 27g
Dinner:
10 oz mushrooms, grilled
½ cup basmati rice, cooked
Nutritional values: Kcal: 398 Protein: 15.5g,
Carbs: 83.3g, Dietary Fiber: 4g, Fats: 1.4g

Day 13
Breakfast:
2 cups grapes
1 large orange
2 kiwis
1 cup lemonade
Nutritional values: Kcal: 319 Protein: 5.3g, Carbs: 80.9g, Dietary Fiber: 12.3g, Fats: 1.8g
Snack:
2 oz hazelnuts
Nutritional values: Kcal: 356 Protein: 8.5g, Carbs: 9.5g, Dietary Fiber: 5.5g, Fats: 34.5g
Lunch:
1 cup mushrooms, grilled
2 large carrots, grilled
1 medium-sized potato, cooked and mashed
1 red bell pepper, grilled
1 tbsp olive oil
Nutritional values: Kcal: 396 Protein: 8.9g, Carbs: 62.7g, Dietary Fiber: 10.5g, Fats: 14.7g
Snack:
2 medium apples
1 cup freshly squeezed orange juice
Nutritional values: Kcal: 344 Protein: 2.9g, Carbs: 87.4g, Dietary Fiber: 11.3g, Fats: 1.3g
Dinner:
3 oz red lentils, cooked
1 carrot cooked
7 oz kale, steamed
2 oz lettuce
Nutritional values: Kcal: 435 Protein: 28.7g, Carbs: 80.6g, Dietary Fiber: 31g, Fats: 1g

Day 14
Breakfast:

1 cup strawberries, fresh

¼ cup almond milk

1 medium apple

1 oz walnuts

Nutritional values: Kcal: 348 Protein: 4.8g, Carbs: 46g, Dietary Fiber: 10.1g, Fats: 19.7g

Snack:

4 large oranges, juiced

Nutritional values: Kcal: 272 Protein: 6.9g, Carbs: 86.4g, Dietary Fiber: 17.6g, Fats: 0.8g

Lunch:

½ cup barley, cooked

¼ cup red lentils, cooked

2 medium-sized tomatoes, fire-roasted

Nutritional values: Kcal: 539 Protein: 26g, Carbs: 106g, Dietary Fiber: 33.5g, Fats: 3.1g

Snack:

1 cup of freshly squeezed lemon juice

1.5 oz walnuts

Nutritional values: Kcal: 321 Protein: 12.2g, Carbs: 9.3g, Dietary Fiber: 3.9g, Fats: 27g

Dinner:

2 oz quinoa, cooked

2 oz white beans, cooked

7 oz spinach, sautéed

1 pear

Nutritional values: Kcal: 524 Protein: 27.4g, Carbs: 98.9g, Dietary Fiber: 21.3g, Fats: 4.9g

Day 15

Breakfast:

¼ cup rolled oats

¼ cup almond milk

1 oz brazil nuts

Nutritional values: Kcal: 401 Protein: 8.2g, Carbs: 20.6g, Dietary Fiber: 5.5g, Fats: 34.6g

Snack:

1 banana

1 oz pecan nuts

Nutritional values: Kcal: 302 Protein: 4.3g, Carbs: 31g, Dietary Fiber: 6.1g, Fats: 20.6g

Lunch:

7 oz artichoke, grilled

1 cup yellow wax beans, cooked

2 tbsp olive oil

2 oz lettuce

Nutritional values: Kcal: 375 Protein: 8.8g, Carbs: 30.4g, Dietary Fiber: 14.8g, Fats: 28.5g

Snack:

10 oz grapefruit

1 medium kiwi

1 oz walnuts

Nutritional values: Kcal: 312 Protein: 9.5g, Carbs: 36.9g, Dietary Fiber: 7.3g, Fats: 17.4g

Dinner:

½ cup green beans, cooked

1 medium-sized carrot, cooked

1 small sweet potato, cooked

½ cup broccoli, grilled

½ cup rice, cooked

Nutritional values: Kcal: 449 Protein: 10.6g, Carbs: 99.3g, Dietary Fiber: 7.8g, Fats: 0.9g

Day 16
Breakfast:

1 cup almond yogurt

2 oz prunes

1 tbsp flaxseed

1 tbsp pumpkin seeds

Nutritional values: Kcal: 394 Protein: 18.6g,
Carbs: 57g, Dietary Fiber: 6.3g, Fats: 9.4g

Snack:

3.5 oz chestnuts, baked

1 medium-sized mango

Nutritional values: Kcal: 395 Protein: 4.4g, Carbs:
93.8g, Dietary Fiber: 5g, Fats: 2.5g

Lunch:

7 oz red bell peppers, grilled

1 tbsp olive oil

7 oz lettuce

1 cup freshly squeezed orange juice

Nutritional values: Kcal: 525 Protein: 11g, Carbs:
94.8g, Dietary Fiber: 13g, Fats: 17g

Snack:

½ medium-sized avocado

1 medium-sized tomato, fresh

2 slices buckwheat bread

1 large orange, juiced

Nutritional values: Kcal: 351 Protein: 5.6g, Carbs:
41.8g, Dietary Fiber: 12.3g, Fats: 25g

Dinner:

3.5 oz chickpeas, cooked

3.5 oz lettuce

7 oz zucchini, grilled

Nutritional values: Kcal: 406 Protein: 22g, Carbs:
69.8g, Dietary Fiber: 20.1g, Fats: 6.5g

Day 17
Breakfast:
3 Wasa crackers
½ cup almond yogurt
1 tbsp chia seeds
7 oz pomegranate seeds
Nutritional values: Kcal: 385 Protein: 14.7g,
Carbs: 53.1g, Dietary Fiber: 11.8g, Fats: 11.1g
Snack:
4 cups blueberries, juiced
Nutritional values: Kcal: 280 Protein: 1.96g,
Carbs: 85.8g, Dietary Fiber: 14.4g, Fats: 1.9g
Lunch:
1 medium-sized zucchini, grilled
2 large red bell peppers, grilled
1 tbsp olive oil
¼ cup basmati rice
1 fig
Nutritional values: Kcal: 405 Protein: 7.5g, Carbs:
64.7g, Dietary Fiber: 6.2g, Fats: 15.1g
Snack:
½ cup strawberries, blended
½ cup blueberries, blended
4 Graham crackers
Nutritional values: Kcal: 301 Protein: 4.9g, Carbs:
59g, Dietary Fiber: 4.8g, Fats: 6.1g
Dinner:
7 oz spinach, steamed
1 red onion, fresh
2 oz pine nuts
Nutritional values: Kcal: 471 Protein: 14.6g,
Carbs: 24.9g, Dietary Fiber: 8.8g, Fats: 39.7g

Day 18
Breakfast
1 large apple, baked
1 cup of raspberries, fresh
1 oz pecan nuts
Nutritional values: Kcal: 377 Protein: 5.1g, Carbs: 49.5g, Dietary Fiber: 16.4g, Fats: 21.4g
Snack:
1 medium-sized grapefruit
1 oz walnuts
Nutritional values: Kcal: 216 Protein: 7.6g, Carbs: 13.2g, Dietary Fiber: 3.3g, Fats: 16.9g
Lunch:
½ cup brown rice, cooked
1 medium-sized carrot, cooked
¼ cup spring onions, fresh
Nutritional values: Kcal: 377 Protein: 8.1g, Carbs: 80.2g, Dietary Fiber: 5.4g, Fats: 2.6g
Snack:
2 Graham crackers
4 medium-sized apricots
10 oz raspberries
Nutritional values: Kcal: 333 Protein: 7.1g, Carbs: 70.7g, Dietary Fiber: 21.9g, Fats: 5.6g
Dinner:
3.5 oz green peas
7 oz spinach, stewed
1 oz almonds, toasted
2 tbsp olive oil
Nutritional values: Kcal: 530 Protein: 17.1g, Carbs: 27.6g, Dietary Fiber: 13g, Fats: 43.4g

Day 19
Breakfast
1 cup of blueberries, fresh
¼ cup of blackberries, fresh
5 walnuts
1 cup of herbal tea
Nutritional values: Kcal: 274 Protein: 8.3g, Carbs: 27.7g, Dietary Fiber: 7.3g, Fats: 17.2g
Snack:
1 cup edamame hummus
½ cup beets, cooked
½ cup shallots, fresh
Nutritional values: Kcal: 471 Protein: 36.6g, Carbs: 50.2g, Dietary Fiber: 12.4g, Fats: 17.6g
Lunch:
7 oz red bell peppers, grilled
1 tbsp olive oil
7 oz lettuce
1 cup freshly squeezed orange juice
Nutritional values: Kcal: 525 Protein: 11g, Carbs: 94.8g, Dietary Fiber: 13g, Fats: 17g
Snack:
1 medium-sized grapefruit
1 oz walnuts
Nutritional values: Kcal: 216 Protein: 7.6g, Carbs: 13.2g, Dietary Fiber: 3.3g, Fats: 16.9g
Dinner:
1 large zucchini, grilled and seasoned with 1 tbsp olive oil
2 slices buckwheat bread
1 pear
Nutritional values: Kcal: 403 Protein: 8.7g, Carbs: 60.7g, Dietary Fiber: 9.2g, Fats: 16.6g

Day 20
Breakfast:
1 cup of blueberries, fresh
¼ cup of blackberries, fresh
5 walnuts
1 cup of herbal tea
Nutritional values: Kcal: 274 Protein: 8.3g, Carbs: 27.7g, Dietary Fiber: 7.3g, Fats: 17.2g
Snack:
1 banana
1 oz pecan nuts
Nutritional values: Kcal: 302 Protein: 4.3g, Carbs: 31g, Dietary Fiber: 6.1g, Fats: 20.6g
Lunch:
1 medium-sized zucchini, grilled
2 large red bell peppers, grilled
1 tbsp olive oil
¼ cup basmati rice
1 fig
Nutritional values: Kcal: 405 Protein: 7.5g, Carbs: 64.7g, Dietary Fiber: 6.2g, Fats: 15.1g
Snack:
4 large oranges, juiced
Nutritional values: Kcal: 272 Protein: 6.9g, Carbs: 86.4g, Dietary Fiber: 17.6g, Fats: 0.8g
Dinner:
5 oz eggplant, steamed
½ cup red lentils, cooked
2 cherry tomatoes, fresh
Nutritional values: Kcal: 419 Protein: 28.3g, Carbs: 75.6g, Dietary Fiber: 37.2g, Fats: 1.8g

Day 21

Breakfast:
1 large baked apple
1 cup of freshly squeezed orange juice
Nutritional values: Kcal: 228 Protein: 2.3g, Carbs: 56.6g, Dietary Fiber: 5.9g, Fats: 0.9g

Snack:
10 oz honeydew melon, fresh
10 oz cherries, fresh
Nutritional values: Kcal: 428 Protein: 2.6g, Carbs: 105.1g, Dietary Fiber: 4g, Fats: 0.6g

Lunch:
5 oz arugula, fresh
½ cup white beans, cooked
1 red onion, fresh
Nutritional values: Kcal: 416 Protein: 28.5g, Carbs: 76.3g, Dietary Fiber: 20g, Fats: 1.9g

Snack:
1 medium-sized mango
4 medium-sized plums
Nutritional values: Kcal: 321 Protein: 4.8g, Carbs: 82g, Dietary Fiber: 8.6g, Fats: 2.1g

Dinner:
1 tomato, fire-roasted
1 zucchini, grilled
7 oz turnip greens, fresh
1 oz walnuts
1 cup freshly squeezed orange juice
Nutritional values: Kcal: 393 Protein: 14.4g, Carbs: 51.7g, Dietary Fiber: 11.7g, Fats: 18.3g

Day 22
Breakfast:
5 large strawberries
1 medium-sized apple
1 oz pecan nuts
1 cup of freshly squeezed orange juice
Nutritional values: Kcal: 454 Protein: 5.9g, Carbs: 67.6g, Dietary Fiber: 10.7g, Fats: 21.4g
Snack:
1 medium-sized grapefruit
1 oz walnuts
Nutritional values: Kcal: 216 Protein: 7.6g, Carbs: 13.2g, Dietary Fiber: 3.3g, Fats: 16.9g
Lunch:
1 tomato, fire-roasted
1 zucchini, grilled
7 oz turnip greens, fresh
1 oz walnuts
1 cup freshly squeezed orange juice
Nutritional values: Kcal: 393 Protein: 14.4g, Carbs: 51.7g, Dietary Fiber: 11.7g, Fats: 18.3g
Snack:
1 banana
1 oz pecan nuts
Nutritional values: Kcal: 302 Protein: 4.3g, Carbs: 31g, Dietary Fiber: 6.1g, Fats: 20.6g
Dinner:
10 oz mushrooms, grilled
4 oz leeks, stewed
3.5 oz radicchio, fresh
1 oz walnuts
Nutritional values: Kcal 420: Protein: 14.3g, Carbs: 62.4g, Dietary Fiber: 10.8g, Fats: 18g

Day23
Breakfast:
1 medium-sized guava
¼ cup rolled oats
¼ cup almond milk
1 oz almonds, toasted
Nutritional values: Kcal: 441 Protein: 12.4g,
Carbs: 36.1g, Dietary Fiber: 11.8g, Fats: 30.7g
Snack:
1 cup of freshly squeezed lemon juice
1.5 oz walnuts
Nutritional values: Kcal: 321 Protein: 12.2g,
Carbs: 9.3g, Dietary Fiber: 3.9g, Fats: 27g
Lunch:
1 cup cauliflower, cooked
1 cup edamame, cooked
Nutritional values: Kcal 401: Protein: 35.1g,
Carbs: 33.6g, Dietary Fiber: 13.2g, Fats: 17.5g
Snack:
1 medium-sized mango
1 large orange, juiced
Nutritional values: Kcal: 287 Protein: 4.5g, Carbs:
71.6g, Dietary Fiber: 9.4g, Fats: 1.5g
Dinner:
5 oz ziti pasta
¼ cup green beans
Nutritional values: Kcal 417: Protein: 16.5g,
Carbs: 79.5g, Dietary Fiber: 0.9g, Fats: 3.3g

Day 24
Breakfast:
1 whole wheat wrap
1 medium-sized tomato, fresh
4 oz avocado, fresh
½ cup spinach, steamed
Nutritional values: Kcal 428: Protein: 7.4g, Carbs: 45.3g, Dietary Fiber: 10.7g, Fats: 25.6g
Snack:
1 oz pecan nuts
Nutritional values: Kcal: 395 Protein: 6.1g, Carbs: 8.1g, Dietary Fiber: 6.1g, Fats: 40.5g
Lunch:
4 oz buckwheat spaghetti
2 oz cherry tomato
2 large plums
Nutritional values: Kcal 397: Protein: 13.8g, Carbs: 79.8g, Dietary Fiber: 2.4g, Fats: 3g
Snack:
10 oz grapefruit
1 medium-sized kiwi
Nutritional values: Kcal: 137 Protein: 2.7g, Carbs: 34g, Dietary Fiber: 5.4g, Fats: 0.7g
Dinner:
7 oz red bell peppers, grilled
1 tbsp olive oil
7 oz lettuce
1 cup freshly squeezed orange juice
Nutritional values: Kcal: 525 Protein: 11g, Carbs: 94.8g, Dietary Fiber: 13g, Fats: 17g

Day 25

Breakfast:

1 large apple, baked

1 cup of raspberries, fresh

1 cup of freshly squeezed orange juice

Nutritional values: Kcal: 292 Protein: 3.8g, Carbs: 71.3g, Dietary Fiber: 13.9g, Fats: 1.7g

Snack:

1 oz pecan nuts

Nutritional values: Kcal: 395 Protein: 6.1g, Carbs: 8.1g, Dietary Fiber: 6.1g, Fats: 40.5g

Lunch:

½ cup black beans, cooked

1 tbsp tahini

Nutritional values: Kcal: 420 Protein: 23.5g, Carbs: 63.7g, Dietary Fiber: 16.1g, Fats: 9.4g

Snack:

1 cup grapes

1 large mango

2 kiwis

Nutritional values: Kcal: 355 Protein: 5.1g, Carbs: 88.1g, Dietary Fiber: 10.4g, Fats: 2.4g

Dinner

10 oz Portobello mushrooms, grilled

½ cup basmati rice, cooked

Nutritional values: Kcal: 398 Protein: 15.5g, Carbs: 83.3g, Dietary Fiber: 4g, Fats: 1.4g

Day26
Breakfast:
2 bananas
1 tbsp pure coconut nectar
1 tbsp flaxseed
1 cup freshly squeezed lemonade
Nutritional values: Kcal: 369 Protein: 5.9g, Carbs: 78.3g, Dietary Fiber: 9.1g, Fats: 4.9g
Snack:
½ cup blueberries
1 oz almonds, toasted
1 oz walnuts
Nutritional values: Kcal: 381 Protein: 13.4g, Carbs: 19.4g, Dietary Fiber: 7.2g, Fats: 31.2g
Lunch:
2 medium-sized corn tortillas
¼ cup black beans, cooked
1 large tomato, diced
7 oz of spinach, steamed
1 medium-sized red bell pepper
Nutritional values: Kcal: 386 Protein: 21.7g, Carbs: 75g, Dietary Fiber: 18.5g, Fats: 3.5g
Snack:
1 peach
2 oz pecan nuts
Nutritional values: Kcal: 454 Protein: 7.5g, Carbs: 22.1g, Dietary Fiber: 8.4g, Fats: 40.9g
Dinner:
4 Roma tomatoes, grilled
½ cup rice, cooked
½ spinach, steamed
Nutritional values: Kcal: 436 Protein: 11.9g, Carbs: 92g, Dietary Fiber: 9.5g, Fats: 3.6g

Day 27

Breakfast:

2 cups grapes

1 large orange

2 kiwis

1 cup lemonade

Nutritional values: Kcal: 319 Protein: 5.3g, Carbs: 80.9g, Dietary Fiber: 12.3g, Fats: 1.8g

Snack:

1 oz pecan nuts

Nutritional values: Kcal: 395 Protein: 6.1g, Carbs: 8.1g, Dietary Fiber: 6.1g, Fats: 40.5g

Lunch:

2 medium-sized corn tortillas

¼ cup black beans, cooked

1 large tomato, diced

7 oz of spinach, steamed

1 medium-sized red bell pepper

Nutritional values: Kcal: 386 Protein: 21.7g, Carbs: 75g, Dietary Fiber: 18.5g, Fats: 3.5g

Snack:

10 oz honeydew melon, fresh

10 oz cherries, fresh

Nutritional values: Kcal: 428 Protein: 2.6g, Carbs: 105.1g, Dietary Fiber: 4g, Fats: 0.6g

Dinner:

5 oz eggplant, steamed

½ cup red lentils, cooked

2 cherry tomatoes, fresh

Nutritional values: Kcal: 419 Protein: 28.3g, Carbs: 75.6g, Dietary Fiber: 37.2g, Fats: 1.8g

Day 28

Breakfast:

10 oz avocado, baked

1 cup of herbal tea

Nutritional values: Kcal: 578 Protein: 5.4g, Carbs: 24.4g, Dietary Fiber: 19g, Fats: 55.3g

Snack:

1 medium-sized apple

Nutritional values: Kcal: 116 Protein: 0.6g, Carbs: 30.8g, Dietary Fiber: 5.4g, Fats: 0.4g

Lunch:

1 cup button mushrooms, grilled

2 large carrots, grilled

1 medium-sized potato, cooked and mashed

1 red bell pepper, grilled

1 tbsp olive oil

Nutritional values: Kcal: 396 Protein: 8.9g, Carbs: 62.7g, Dietary Fiber: 10.5g, Fats: 14.7g

Snack:

1 cup of freshly squeezed lemon juice

1.5 oz walnuts

Nutritional values: Kcal: 321 Protein: 12.2g, Carbs: 9.3g, Dietary Fiber: 3.9g, Fats: 27g

Dinner:

10 oz Portobello mushrooms, grilled

½ cup basmati rice, cooked

Nutritional values: Kcal: 398 Protein: 15.5g, Carbs: 83.3g, Dietary Fiber: 4g, Fats: 1.4g

Day 29
Breakfast:
1 cup almond yogurt
1 tbsp chia seeds
3 figs
1 cup of black coffee
Nutritional values: Kcal: 457 Protein: 22.1g,
Carbs: 64.2g, Dietary Fiber: 16g, Fats: 13.1g
Snack:
1 oz pecan nuts
Nutritional values: Kcal: 395 Protein: 6.1g, Carbs:
8.1g, Dietary Fiber: 6.1g, Fats: 40.5g
Lunch:
½ cup brown rice, cooked
1 medium-sized carrot, cooked
¼ cup spring onions, fresh
Nutritional values: Kcal: 377 Protein: 8.1g, Carbs:
80.2g, Dietary Fiber: 5.4g, Fats: 2.6g
Snack:
1 banana
1 oz pecan nuts
Nutritional values: Kcal: 302 Protein: 4.3g, Carbs:
31g, Dietary Fiber: 6.1g, Fats: 20.6g
Dinner:
½ cup green beans, cooked
1 medium-sized carrot, cooked
1 small sweet potato, cooked
½ cup broccoli, grilled
½ cup rice, cooked
Nutritional values: Kcal: 449 Protein: 10.6g,
Carbs: 99.3g, Dietary Fiber: 7.8g, Fats: 0.9g

Day 30

Breakfast:

1 large apple, baked

1 cup of raspberries, fresh

1 cup of freshly squeezed orange juice

Nutritional values: Kcal: 292 Protein: 3.8g, Carbs: 71.3g, Dietary Fiber: 13.9g, Fats: 1.7g

Snack:

10 oz honeydew melon, fresh

10 oz cherries, fresh

Nutritional values: Kcal: 428 Protein: 2.6g, Carbs: 105.1g, Dietary Fiber: 4g, Fats: 0.6g

Lunch:

3.5 oz buckwheat noodles, cooked and seasoned with one tablespoon of olive oil

2 oz spring onions, steamed

3.5 oz kale, steamed

Nutritional values: Kcal: 512 Protein: 16.1g, Carbs: 83.1g, Dietary Fiber: 12.7g, Fats: 17.2g

Snack:

10 oz grilled red peppers

10 oz melon

4 pecans

1 cup of herbal tea

Nutritional values: Kcal: 212 Protein: 7.7g, Carbs: 48.6g, Dietary Fiber: 6.8g, Fats: 1.8g

Dinner:

3 oz red lentils, cooked

1 carrot cooked

7 oz kale, steamed

2 oz lettuce

Nutritional values: Kcal: 435 Protein: 28.7g, Carbs: 80.6g, Dietary Fiber: 31g, Fats: 1g

Day 31
Breakfast:
1 cup of blueberries, fresh
¼ cup of blackberries, fresh
5 walnuts
1 cup of herbal tea
Nutritional values: Kcal: 274 Protein: 8.3g, Carbs: 27.7g, Dietary Fiber: 7.3g, Fats: 17.2g
Snack:
7 oz avocado, baked
Nutritional values: Kcal: 405 Protein: 3.8g, Carbs: 17.1g, Dietary Fiber: 13.3g, Fats: 38.7g
Lunch:
5 oz arugula, fresh
½ cup white beans, cooked
1 red onion, fresh
Nutritional values: Kcal: 416 Protein: 28.5g, Carbs: 76.3g, Dietary Fiber: 20g, Fats: 1.9g
Snack:
2 peaches
1 oz walnuts
Nutritional values: Kcal: 293 Protein: 9.6g, Carbs: 30.8g, Dietary Fiber: 6.5g, Fats: 17.5g
Dinner:
7 oz sweet potato, baked
¼ cup kidney beans, cooked
1 oz buckwheat bread
1 cup of herbal tea
Nutritional values: Kcal: 410 Protein: 16.5g, Carbs: 83.6g, Dietary Fiber: 14.3g, Fats: 1.8g

Day 32
Breakfast:

1 banana

4 oz cherries

1 buckwheat wrap

Nutritional values: Kcal: 406 Protein: 5.5g, Carbs: 88.9g, Dietary Fiber: 5g, Fats: 3.6g

Snack:

4 oz strawberries

4 Graham crackers

1 large orange, juiced

Nutritional values: Kcal: 360 Protein: 6.3g, Carbs: 73.3g, Dietary Fiber: 8.3g, Fats: 6.2g

Lunch:

½ cup button mushrooms, grilled

1 cup celery, fresh

½ cup black beans, cooked

1 peach

Nutritional values: Kcal: 413 Protein: 24.1g, Carbs: 78.6g, Dietary Fiber: 19g, Fats: 2g

Snack:

½ cup blueberries

1 oz almonds, toasted

1 oz walnuts

Nutritional values: Kcal: 381 Protein: 13.4g, Carbs: 19.4g, Dietary Fiber: 7.2g, Fats: 31.2g

Dinner:

½ small eggplant, grilled

½ cup kidney beans, cooked

2 oz raspberries

Nutritional values: Kcal: 397 Protein: 23.6g, Carbs: 76.6g, Dietary Fiber: 25.8g, Fats: 1.8g

Day 33

Breakfast:

1 banana

1 oz pecan nuts

Nutritional values: Kcal: 302 Protein: 4.3g, Carbs: 31g, Dietary Fiber: 6.1g, Fats: 20.6g

Snack:

2 oz almonds, toasted

1 medium-sized apple

Nutritional values: Kcal: 444 Protein: 12.6g, Carbs: 43g, Dietary Fiber: 12.5g, Fats: 28.8g

Lunch:

5 oz buckwheat noodles, cooked

2 oz tomato paste

1 small artichoke, steamed

4 dates

Nutritional values: Kcal: 396 Protein: 13.9g, Carbs: 84.7g, Dietary Fiber: 13.6g, Fats: 3.5g

Snack:

3.5 oz chestnuts, baked

1 medium-sized mango

Nutritional values: Kcal: 395 Protein: 4.4g, Carbs: 93.8g, Dietary Fiber: 5g, Fats: 2.5g

Dinner:

3 oz red lentils, cooked

1 carrot cooked

7 oz kale, steamed

2 oz lettuce

Nutritional values: Kcal: 435 Protein: 28.7g, Carbs: 80.6g, Dietary Fiber: 31g, Fats: 1g

Day 34
Breakfast:
1 cup of strawberries, fresh
½ cup raspberries, fresh
5 almonds, toasted
½ cup almond yogurt
1 cup of herbal tea
Nutritional values: Kcal: 200 Protein: 10g, Carbs: 28.3g, Dietary Fiber: 7.6g, Fats: 5.3g
Snack:
10 oz avocado, baked
1 cup of herbal tea
Nutritional values: Kcal: 578 Protein: 5.4g, Carbs: 24.4g, Dietary Fiber: 19g, Fats: 55.3g
Lunch:
½ cup brown rice, cooked
1 medium-sized carrot, cooked
¼ cup spring onions, fresh
Nutritional values: Kcal: 377 Protein: 8.1g, Carbs: 80.2g, Dietary Fiber: 5.4g, Fats: 2.6g
Snack:
1 medium-sized mango
4 medium-sized plums
Nutritional values: Kcal: 321 Protein: 4.8g, Carbs: 82g, Dietary Fiber: 8.6g, Fats: 2.1g
Dinner:
7 oz buckwheat noodles, cooked and seasoned with one tablespoon of olive oil
2 oz spring onions, steamed
Nutritional values: Kcal: 412 Protein: 10.1g, Carbs: 54.1g, Dietary Fiber: 3.8g, Fats: 18.2g

Day 35
Breakfast:
1 large baked apple
1 cup of freshly squeezed orange juice
Nutritional values: Kcal: 228 Protein: 2.3g, Carbs: 56.6g, Dietary Fiber: 5.9g, Fats: 0.9g
Snack:
3.5 oz walnuts
Nutritional values: Kcal: 613 Protein: 23.9g, Carbs: 9.8g, Dietary Fiber: 6.8g, Fats: 58.5g
Lunch:
5 oz shiitake mushrooms, grilled
1 white onion, grilled
1 tbsp olive oil
Nutritional values: Kcal: 241 Protein: 3.4g, Carbs: 29.8g, Dietary Fiber: 5.3g, Fats: 14.4g
Snack:
1 medium-sized grapefruit
1 oz walnuts
Nutritional values: Kcal: 257 Protein: 8.4g, Carbs: 23.5g, Dietary Fiber: 4.8g, Fats: 17g
Dinner:
7 oz sweet potato, baked
¼ cup kidney beans, cooked
1 oz buckwheat bread
1 cup of herbal tea
Nutritional values: Kcal: 410 Protein: 16.5g, Carbs: 83.6g, Dietary Fiber: 14.3g, Fats: 1.8g

Day 36
Breakfast:
2 bananas
1 tbsp pure coconut nectar
1 tbsp flaxseed
1 cup freshly squeezed lemonade
Nutritional values: Kcal: 369 Protein: 5.9g, Carbs: 78.3g, Dietary Fiber: 9.1g, Fats: 4.9g
Snack:
1 banana
1 oz pecan nuts
Nutritional values: Kcal: 302 Protein: 4.3g, Carbs: 31g, Dietary Fiber: 6.1g, Fats: 20.6g
Lunch:
1 cup edamame hummus
½ cup beets, cooked
½ cup shallots, fresh
Nutritional values: Kcal: 471 Protein: 36.6g, Carbs: 50.2g, Dietary Fiber: 12.4g, Fats: 17.6g
Snack:
7 oz chestnuts, baked
Nutritional values: Kcal: 389 Protein: 3.2g, Carbs: 87.7g, Dietary Fiber: 8.7g, Fats: 2.5g
Dinner:
1 tomato, fire-roasted
1 zucchini, grilled
7 oz turnip greens, fresh
1 oz walnuts
1 cup freshly squeezed orange juice
Nutritional values: Kcal: 393 Protein: 14.4g, Carbs: 51.7g, Dietary Fiber: 11.7g, Fats: 18.3g

Day 37
Breakfast:
1 large baked apple
1 cup of freshly squeezed orange juice
Nutritional values: Kcal: 228 Protein: 2.3g, Carbs: 56.6g, Dietary Fiber: 5.9g, Fats: 0.9g
Snack:
1 red bell pepper
1 yellow bell pepper
1 green bell pepper
1 cup avocado chunks
Nutritional values: Kcal: 412 Protein: 6.4g, Carbs: 39.6g, Dietary Fiber: 14.6g, Fats: 29.4g
Lunch:
2 cup butternut squash, cooked
1 cup brussel sprouts, cooked
1 cup leeks, cooked
1 tbsp olive oil
Nutritional values: Kcal: 338 Protein: 71g, Carbs: 53.3g, Dietary Fiber: 10.5g, Fats: 14.8g
Snack:
1 oz pecan nuts
Nutritional values: Kcal: 395 Protein: 6.1g, Carbs: 8.1g, Dietary Fiber: 6.1g, Fats: 40.5g
Dinner:
5 oz arugula, fresh
½ cup white beans, cooked
1 red onion, fresh
Nutritional values: Kcal: 416 Protein: 28.5g, Carbs: 76.3g, Dietary Fiber: 20g, Fats: 1.9g

Day 38
Breakfast:

2 apples, baked

1 cup of herbal tea

Nutritional values: Kcal: 234 Protein: 1.2g, Carbs: 62.1g, Dietary Fiber: 10.8g, Fats: 0.8g

Snack:

7 oz avocado, baked

Nutritional values: Kcal: 405 Protein: 3.8g, Carbs: 17.1g, Dietary Fiber: 13.3g, Fats: 38.7g

Lunch:

7 oz hummus

1 oz buckwheat bread

7 oz carrot sticks

Nutritional values: Kcal: 486 Protein: 19.5g, Carbs: 62.2g, Dietary Fiber: 17.5g, Fats: 20g

Snack:

1 medium-sized mango

4 medium-sized plums

Nutritional values: Kcal: 321 Protein: 4.8g, Carbs: 82g, Dietary Fiber: 8.6g, Fats: 2.1g

Dinner:

1 cup button mushrooms, grilled

2 large carrots, grilled

1 medium-sized potato, cooked and mashed

1 red bell pepper, grilled

1 tbsp olive oil

Nutritional values: Kcal: 396 Protein: 8.9g, Carbs: 62.7g, Dietary Fiber: 10.5g, Fats: 14.7g

Day 39
Breakfast:
1 large apple, baked
1 cup of raspberries, fresh
1 oz pecan nuts
Nutritional values: Kcal: 377 Protein: 5.1g, Carbs: 49.5g, Dietary Fiber: 16.4g, Fats: 21.4g
Snack:
1 avocado, juiced
Nutritional values: Kcal: 268 Protein: 4g, Carbs: 17.1g, Dietary Fiber: 13.5g, Fats: 29.4g
Lunch:
7 oz spinach, steamed
1 red onion, fresh
2 oz pine nuts
Nutritional values: Kcal: 471 Protein: 14.6g, Carbs: 24.9g, Dietary Fiber: 8.8g, Fats: 39.7g
Snack:
10 oz honeydew melon, fresh
10 oz cherries, fresh
Nutritional values: Kcal: 428 Protein: 2.6g, Carbs: 105.1g, Dietary Fiber: 4g, Fats: 0.6g
Dinner:
10 oz Portobello mushrooms, grilled
½ cup basmati rice, cooked
Nutritional values: Kcal: 398 Protein: 15.5g, Carbs: 83.3g, Dietary Fiber: 4g, Fats: 1.4g

Day 40
Breakfast:

1 large apple, baked

1 cup of raspberries, fresh

1 cup of freshly squeezed orange juice

Nutritional values: Kcal: 292 Protein: 3.8g, Carbs: 71.3g, Dietary Fiber: 13.9g, Fats: 1.7g

Snack:

1 peach

2 oz pecan nuts

Nutritional values: Kcal: 454 Protein: 7.5g, Carbs: 22.1g, Dietary Fiber: 8.4g, Fats: 40.9g

Lunch:

7 oz sweet potato, baked

¼ cup kidney beans, cooked

1 oz buckwheat bread

1 cup of herbal tea

Nutritional values: Kcal: 410 Protein: 16.5g, Carbs: 83.6g, Dietary Fiber: 14.3g, Fats: 1.8g

Snack:

1 kiwi

1.5 oz almonds, toasted

Nutritional values: Kcal: 292 Protein: 9.9g, Carbs: 20.2g, Dietary Fiber: 7.6g, Fats: 21.7g

Dinner:

10oz shiitake mushrooms, grilled

4 oz leeks, stewed

3.5 oz radicchio, fresh

1 oz walnuts

Nutritional values: Kcal 420: Protein: 14.3g, Carbs: 62.4g, Dietary Fiber: 10.8g, Fats: 18g

Day 41
Breakfast:
¼ cup rolled oats
¼ cup almond milk
1 oz brazil nuts
Nutritional values: Kcal: 401 Protein: 8.2g, Carbs: 20.6g, Dietary Fiber: 5.5g, Fats: 34.6g
Snack:
1 medium-sized mango
4 medium-sized plums
Nutritional values: Kcal: 321 Protein: 4.8g, Carbs: 82g, Dietary Fiber: 8.6g, Fats: 2.1g
Lunch:
3.5 oz green peas
7 oz spinach, stewed
1 oz almonds, toasted
2 tbsp olive oil
Nutritional values: Kcal: 530 Protein: 17.1g, Carbs: 27.6g, Dietary Fiber: 13g, Fats: 43.4g
Snack:
1 cup of freshly squeezed orange juice
Nutritional values: Kcal: 112 Protein: 1.7g, Carbs: 25.8g, Dietary Fiber: 0.5g, Fats: 0.5g
Dinner:
7 oz spinach, steamed
1 red onion, fresh
2 oz pine nuts
Nutritional values: Kcal: 471 Protein: 14.6g, Carbs: 24.9g, Dietary Fiber: 8.8g, Fats: 39.7g

Day 42

Breakfast

1 large apple, baked
1 cup of raspberries, fresh
1 cup of freshly squeezed orange juice
Nutritional values: Kcal: 292 Protein: 3.8g, Carbs: 71.3g, Dietary Fiber: 13.9g, Fats: 1.7g

Snack:

1 oz pecan nuts
Nutritional values: Kcal: 395 Protein: 6.1g, Carbs: 8.1g, Dietary Fiber: 6.1g, Fats: 40.5g

Lunch:

½ cup leek, cooked
1 medium-sized potato, cooked
½ cup shallots, cooked
1 tbsp olive oil
Nutritional values: Kcal: 369 Protein: 7g, Carbs: 56.9g, Dietary Fiber: 5.5g, Fats: 14.4g

Snack:

3.5 oz walnuts
Nutritional values: Kcal: 613 Protein: 23.9g, Carbs: 9.8g, Dietary Fiber: 6.8g, Fats: 58.5g

Dinner:

2 slices buckwheat bread
1 medium-sized tomato, fresh
1 small cucumber
1 red onion, fresh
1 tbsp olive oil
Nutritional values: Kcal: 268 Protein: 5.1g, Carbs: 32.7g, Dietary Fiber: 5g, Fats: 15.1g

Day 43

Breakfast
1 cup almond yogurt
7 oz pineapple chunks
1 large orange
1 cup of herbal tea
Nutritional values: Kcal: 362 Protein: 16.8g,
Carbs: 65.4g, Dietary Fiber: 7.2g, Fats: 3.5g
Snack:
7 oz cherries
Nutritional values: Kcal: 228 Protein: 0.7g, Carbs:
55.6g, Dietary Fiber: 1.2g, Fats: 0.1g
Lunch:
½ cup barley, cooked
¼ cup red lentils, cooked
2 medium-sized tomatoes, fire-roasted
Nutritional values: Kcal: 539 Protein: 26g, Carbs:
106g, Dietary Fiber: 33.5g, Fats: 3.1g
Snack:
1 cup of freshly squeezed lemon juice
1.5 oz walnuts
Nutritional values: Kcal: 321 Protein: 12.2g,
Carbs: 9.3g, Dietary Fiber: 3.9g, Fats: 27g
Dinner:
7 oz artichoke, grilled
1 cup yellow wax beans, cooked
2 tbsp olive oil
2 oz lettuce
Nutritional values: Kcal: 375 Protein: 8.8g, Carbs:
30.4g, Dietary Fiber: 14.8g, Fats: 28.5g

Day 44

Breakfast:
1 cup strawberries, fresh
¼ cup almond milk
1 medium-sized apple
1 oz walnuts
Nutritional values: Kcal: 348 Protein: 4.8g, Carbs: 46g, Dietary Fiber: 10.1g, Fats: 19.7g
Snack:
10 oz honeydew melon, fresh
10 oz cherries, fresh
Nutritional values: Kcal: 428 Protein: 2.6g, Carbs: 105.1g, Dietary Fiber: 4g, Fats: 0.6g
Lunch:
3.5 oz buckwheat pasta, cooked
1 large tomato
3.5 oz lettuce
Nutritional values: Kcal: 330 Protein: 13.2g, Carbs: 63.9g, Dietary Fiber: 2.7g, Fats: 2.8g
Snack:
10 oz grapefruit
1 medium-sized kiwi
1 oz walnuts
Nutritional values: Kcal: 312 Protein: 9.5g, Carbs: 36.9g, Dietary Fiber: 7.3g, Fats: 17.4g
Dinner:
7 oz buckwheat noodles, cooked and seasoned with one tablespoon of olive oil
2 oz spring onions, steamed
Nutritional values: Kcal: 412 Protein: 10.1g, Carbs: 54.1g, Dietary Fiber: 3.8g, Fats: 18.2g

Day 45

Breakfast:
1 cup almond yogurt
1 tbsp chia seeds
3 figs
1 cup of black coffee
Nutritional values: Kcal: 457 Protein: 22.1g,
Carbs: 64.2g, Dietary Fiber: 16g, Fats: 13.1g
Snack:
4 cups blueberries, juiced
Nutritional values: Kcal: 280 Protein: 1.96g,
Carbs: 85.8g, Dietary Fiber: 14.4g, Fats: 1.9g
Lunch:
7 oz artichoke
½ cup kidney beans
1 tbsp extra virgin olive oil
Nutritional values: Kcal: 523 Protein: 27.2g,
Carbs: 77.2g, Dietary Fiber: 24.7g, Fats: 15.3g
Snack:
1 avocado, juiced
Nutritional values: Kcal: 268 Protein: 4g, Carbs:
17.1g, Dietary Fiber: 13.5g, Fats: 29.4g
Dinner:
7 oz arugula
1 cup raspberries
1 oz walnuts
1 cup freshly squeezed orange juice
Nutritional values: Kcal: 401 Protein: 15.1g,
Carbs: 50.5g, Dietary Fiber: 13.6g, Fats: 19.3g

Day 46
Breakfast:
2 bananas
1 tbsp pure coconut nectar
1 tbsp flaxseed
1 cup freshly squeezed lemonade
Nutritional values: Kcal: 369 Protein: 5.9g, Carbs: 78.3g, Dietary Fiber: 9.1g, Fats: 4.9g
Snack:
1 cup of freshly squeezed lemon juice
1.5 oz walnuts
Nutritional values: Kcal: 321 Protein: 12.2g, Carbs: 9.3g, Dietary Fiber: 3.9g, Fats: 27g
Lunch:
5 oz eggplant, steamed
½ cup red lentils, cooked
2 cherry tomatoes, fresh
Nutritional values: Kcal: 419 Protein: 28.3g, Carbs: 75.6g, Dietary Fiber: 37.2g, Fats: 1.8g
Snack:
7 oz grapes
1 oz pecan nuts
Nutritional values: Kcal: 330 Protein: 4.3g, Carbs: 38.1g, Dietary Fiber: 4.8g, Fats: 20.9g
Dinner:
3 oz red lentils, cooked
1 carrot cooked
7 oz kale, steamed
2 oz lettuce
Nutritional values: Kcal: 435 Protein: 28.7g, Carbs: 80.6g, Dietary Fiber: 31g, Fats: 1g

Day 47

Breakfast:

½ cup quinoa, cooked

3 tbsp raisins

¼ cup coconut milk

1 cup of black coffee

Nutritional values: Kcal: 532 Protein: 14.2g, Carbs: 79.4g, Dietary Fiber: 8.3g, Fats: 19.6g

Snack:

1 cup cantaloupe, fresh

6 dates

Nutritional values: Kcal: 193 Protein: 2.5g, Carbs: 50.1g, Dietary Fiber: 5.4g, Fats: 0.5g

Lunch:

10oz shiitake mushrooms, grilled

4 oz leeks, stewed

3.5 oz radicchio, fresh

1 oz walnuts

Nutritional values: Kcal 420: Protein: 14.3g, Carbs: 62.4g, Dietary Fiber: 10.8g, Fats: 18g

Snack:

4 medium-sized apricots

10 oz raspberries

Nutritional values: Kcal: 214 Protein: 5.2g, Carbs: 49.2g, Dietary Fiber: 21.1g, Fats: 2.7g

Dinner:

4 Roma tomatoes, grilled

½ cup rice, cooked

½ spinach, steamed

Nutritional values: Kcal: 436 Protein: 11.9g, Carbs: 92g, Dietary Fiber: 9.5g, Fats: 3.6g

Day 48

Breakfast:

2 large oranges, broiled

2 oz walnuts

1 cup of herbal tea

Nutritional values: Kcal: 523 Protein: 17.1g, Carbs: 48.9g, Dietary Fiber: 12.7g, Fats: 33.9g

Snack:

1 avocado, juiced

Nutritional values: Kcal: 268 Protein: 4g, Carbs: 17.1g, Dietary Fiber: 13.5g, Fats: 29.4g

Lunch:

3.5 oz green peas

7 oz spinach, stewed

1 oz almonds, toasted

2 tbsp olive oil

Nutritional values: Kcal: 530 Protein: 17.1g, Carbs: 27.6g, Dietary Fiber: 13g, Fats: 43.4g

Snack:

1 medium-sized orange

Nutritional values: Kcal: 86 Protein: 1.7g, Carbs: 21.6g, Dietary Fiber: 4.4g, Fats: 0.2g

Dinner:

½ cup brown rice, cooked

1 medium-sized carrot, cooked

¼ cup spring onions, fresh

Nutritional values: Kcal: 377 Protein: 8.1g, Carbs: 80.2g, Dietary Fiber: 5.4g, Fats: 2.6g

Day 49

Breakfast:

1 large apple, baked

1 cup of raspberries, fresh

1 oz pecan nuts

Nutritional values: Kcal: 377 Protein: 5.1g, Carbs: 49.5g, Dietary Fiber: 16.4g, Fats: 21.4g

Snack:

2 Graham crackers

4 medium-sized apricots

10 oz raspberries

Nutritional values: Kcal: 333 Protein: 7.1g, Carbs: 70.7g, Dietary Fiber: 21.9g, Fats: 5.6g

Lunch:

1 medium-sized zucchini, grilled

2 large red bell peppers, grilled

1 tbsp olive oil

¼ cup basmati rice

1 fig

Nutritional values: Kcal: 405 Protein: 7.5g, Carbs: 64.7g, Dietary Fiber: 6.2g, Fats: 15.1g

Snack:

½ medium-sized avocado

1 medium-sized tomato, fresh

2 slices buckwheat bread

1 large orange, juiced

Nutritional values: Kcal: 351 Protein: 5.6g, Carbs: 41.8g, Dietary Fiber: 12.3g, Fats: 25g

Dinner

7 oz red bell peppers, grilled

1 tbsp olive oil

7 oz lettuce

1 cup freshly squeezed orange juice

Nutritional values: Kcal: 525 Protein: 11g, Carbs: 94.8g, Dietary Fiber: 13g, Fats: 17g

Day 50
Breakfast:
5 large strawberries
1 medium-sized apple
1 oz pecan nuts
1 cup of freshly squeezed orange juice
Nutritional values: Kcal: 454 Protein: 5.9g, Carbs: 67.6g, Dietary Fiber: 10.7g, Fats: 21.4g
Snack:
4 large oranges, juiced
Nutritional values: Kcal: 272 Protein: 6.9g, Carbs: 86.4g, Dietary Fiber: 17.6g, Fats: 0.8g
Lunch:
2 oz quinoa, cooked
2 oz white beans, cooked
7 oz spinach, sautéed
1 pear
Nutritional values: Kcal: 524 Protein: 27.4g, Carbs: 98.9g, Dietary Fiber: 21.3g, Fats: 4.9g
Snack:
3.5 oz cherries
Nutritional values: Kcal: 114 Protein: 0.4g, Carbs: 27.8g, Dietary Fiber: 0.6g, Fats: 0.1g
Dinner:
10 oz button mushrooms, grilled
4 oz leeks, stewed
3.5 oz radicchio, fresh
1 oz walnuts
Nutritional values: Kcal 420: Protein: 14.3g, Carbs: 62.4g, Dietary Fiber: 10.8g, Fats: 18g

Day 51:

Breakfast

1 cup almond yogurt
7 oz pineapple chunks
1 large orange
1 cup of herbal tea
Nutritional values: Kcal: 362 Protein: 16.8g,
Carbs: 65.4g, Dietary Fiber: 7.2g, Fats: 3.5g

Snack:

2 slices buckwheat bread
1 medium-sized tomato, fresh
1 small cucumber
1 red onion, fresh
1 tbsp olive oil
Nutritional values: Kcal: 268 Protein: 5.1g, Carbs:
32.7g, Dietary Fiber: 5g, Fats: 15.1g

Lunch:

3.5 oz enoki mushrooms, grilled
7 oz shiitake mushrooms, grilled
3.5 oz shishito peppers, grilled
2 oz buckwheat bread
Nutritional values: Kcal: 550 Protein: 20.6g,
Carbs: 127g, Dietary Fiber: 34.3g, Fats: 5.8g

Snack:

7 oz cherries
Nutritional values: Kcal: 228 Protein: 0.7g, Carbs:
55.6g, Dietary Fiber: 1.2g, Fats: 0.1g

Dinner:

½ cup black beans, cooked
1 tbsp tahini
Nutritional values: Kcal: 420 Protein: 23.5g,
Carbs: 63.7g, Dietary Fiber: 16.1g, Fats: 9.4g

Day 52:
Breakfast:
1 cup almond yogurt
1 tbsp chia seeds
3 figs
1 cup of black coffee
Nutritional values: Kcal: 457 Protein: 22.1g,
Carbs: 64.2g, Dietary Fiber: 16g, Fats: 13.1g
Snack:
½ cup leek, cooked
1 medium-sized potato, cooked
½ cup shallots, cooked
1 tbsp olive oil
Nutritional values: Kcal: 369 Protein: 7g, Carbs:
56.9g, Dietary Fiber: 5.5g, Fats: 14.4g
Lunch:
1 cup edamame hummus
½ cup beets, cooked
½ cup shallots, fresh
Nutritional values: Kcal: 471 Protein: 36.6g,
Carbs: 50.2g, Dietary Fiber: 12.4g, Fats: 17.6g
Snack:
1 cup of freshly squeezed lemon juice
1.5 oz walnuts
Nutritional values: Kcal: 321 Protein: 12.2g,
Carbs: 9.3g, Dietary Fiber: 3.9g, Fats: 27g
Dinner:
10 oz mushrooms, grilled
½ cup basmati rice, cooked
Nutritional values: Kcal: 398 Protein: 15.5g,
Carbs: 83.3g, Dietary Fiber: 4g, Fats: 1.4g

Day 53
Breakfast:
2 cups grapes
1 large orange
2 kiwis
1 cup lemonade
Nutritional values: Kcal: 319 Protein: 5.3g, Carbs: 80.9g, Dietary Fiber: 12.3g, Fats: 1.8g
Snack:
2 oz hazelnuts
Nutritional values: Kcal: 356 Protein: 8.5g, Carbs: 9.5g, Dietary Fiber: 5.5g, Fats: 34.5g
Lunch:
1 cup mushrooms, grilled
2 large carrots, grilled
1 medium-sized potato, cooked and mashed
1 red bell pepper, grilled
1 tbsp olive oil
Nutritional values: Kcal: 396 Protein: 8.9g, Carbs: 62.7g, Dietary Fiber: 10.5g, Fats: 14.7g
Snack:
2 medium apples
1 cup freshly squeezed orange juice
Nutritional values: Kcal: 344 Protein: 2.9g, Carbs: 87.4g, Dietary Fiber: 11.3g, Fats: 1.3g
Dinner:
3 oz red lentils, cooked
1 carrot cooked
7 oz kale, steamed
2 oz lettuce
Nutritional values: Kcal: 435 Protein: 28.7g, Carbs: 80.6g, Dietary Fiber: 31g, Fats: 1g

Day 54
Breakfast:
1 cup strawberries, fresh
¼ cup almond milk
1 medium apple
1 oz walnuts
Nutritional values: Kcal: 348 Protein: 4.8g, Carbs: 46g, Dietary Fiber: 10.1g, Fats: 19.7g
Snack:
4 large oranges, juiced
Nutritional values: Kcal: 272 Protein: 6.9g, Carbs: 86.4g, Dietary Fiber: 17.6g, Fats: 0.8g
Lunch:
½ cup barley, cooked
¼ cup red lentils, cooked
2 medium-sized tomatoes, fire-roasted
Nutritional values: Kcal: 539 Protein: 26g, Carbs: 106g, Dietary Fiber: 33.5g, Fats: 3.1g
Snack:
1 cup of freshly squeezed lemon juice
1.5 oz walnuts
Nutritional values: Kcal: 321 Protein: 12.2g, Carbs: 9.3g, Dietary Fiber: 3.9g, Fats: 27g
Dinner:
2 oz quinoa, cooked
2 oz white beans, cooked
7 oz spinach, sautéed
1 pear
Nutritional values: Kcal: 524 Protein: 27.4g, Carbs: 98.9g, Dietary Fiber: 21.3g, Fats: 4.9g

Day 55
Breakfast:
¼ cup rolled oats
¼ cup almond milk
1 oz brazil nuts
Nutritional values: Kcal: 401 Protein: 8.2g, Carbs: 20.6g, Dietary Fiber: 5.5g, Fats: 34.6g
Snack:
1 banana
1 oz pecan nuts
Nutritional values: Kcal: 302 Protein: 4.3g, Carbs: 31g, Dietary Fiber: 6.1g, Fats: 20.6g
Lunch:
7 oz artichoke, grilled
1 cup yellow wax beans, cooked
2 tbsp olive oil
2 oz lettuce
Nutritional values: Kcal: 375 Protein: 8.8g, Carbs: 30.4g, Dietary Fiber: 14.8g, Fats: 28.5g
Snack:
10 oz grapefruit
1 medium kiwi
1 oz walnuts
Nutritional values: Kcal: 312 Protein: 9.5g, Carbs: 36.9g, Dietary Fiber: 7.3g, Fats: 17.4g
Dinner:
½ cup green beans, cooked
1 medium-sized carrot, cooked
1 small sweet potato, cooked
½ cup broccoli, grilled
½ cup rice, cooked
Nutritional values: Kcal: 449 Protein: 10.6g, Carbs: 99.3g, Dietary Fiber: 7.8g, Fats: 0.9g

Day 56
Breakfast:

1 cup almond yogurt

2 oz prunes

1 tbsp flaxseed

1 tbsp pumpkin seeds

Nutritional values: Kcal: 394 Protein: 18.6g, Carbs: 57g, Dietary Fiber: 6.3g, Fats: 9.4g

Snack:

3.5 oz chestnuts, baked

1 medium-sized mango

Nutritional values: Kcal: 395 Protein: 4.4g, Carbs: 93.8g, Dietary Fiber: 5g, Fats: 2.5g

Lunch:

7 oz red bell peppers, grilled

1 tbsp olive oil

7 oz lettuce

1 cup freshly squeezed orange juice

Nutritional values: Kcal: 525 Protein: 11g, Carbs: 94.8g, Dietary Fiber: 13g, Fats: 17g

Snack:

½ medium-sized avocado

1 medium-sized tomato, fresh

2 slices buckwheat bread

1 large orange, juiced

Nutritional values: Kcal: 351 Protein: 5.6g, Carbs: 41.8g, Dietary Fiber: 12.3g, Fats: 25g

Dinner:

3.5 oz chickpeas, cooked

3.5 oz lettuce

7 oz zucchini, grilled

Nutritional values: Kcal: 406 Protein: 22g, Carbs: 69.8g, Dietary Fiber: 20.1g, Fats: 6.5g

Day 57
Breakfast:
3 Wasa crackers
½ cup almond yogurt
1 tbsp chia seeds
7 oz pomegranate seeds
Nutritional values: Kcal: 385 Protein: 14.7g,
Carbs: 53.1g, Dietary Fiber: 11.8g, Fats: 11.1g
Snack:
4 cups blueberries, juiced
Nutritional values: Kcal: 280 Protein: 1.96g,
Carbs: 85.8g, Dietary Fiber: 14.4g, Fats: 1.9g
Lunch:
1 medium-sized zucchini, grilled
2 large red bell peppers, grilled
1 tbsp olive oil
¼ cup basmati rice
1 fig
Nutritional values: Kcal: 405 Protein: 7.5g, Carbs:
64.7g, Dietary Fiber: 6.2g, Fats: 15.1g
Snack:
½ cup strawberries, blended
½ cup blueberries, blended
4 Graham crackers
Nutritional values: Kcal: 301 Protein: 4.9g, Carbs:
59g, Dietary Fiber: 4.8g, Fats: 6.1g
Dinner:
7 oz spinach, steamed
1 red onion, fresh
2 oz pine nuts
Nutritional values: Kcal: 471 Protein: 14.6g,
Carbs: 24.9g, Dietary Fiber: 8.8g, Fats: 39.7g

Day 58

Breakfast

1 large apple, baked
1 cup of raspberries, fresh
1 oz pecan nuts
Nutritional values: Kcal: 377 Protein: 5.1g, Carbs: 49.5g, Dietary Fiber: 16.4g, Fats: 21.4g

Snack:

1 medium-sized grapefruit
1 oz walnuts
Nutritional values: Kcal: 216 Protein: 7.6g, Carbs: 13.2g, Dietary Fiber: 3.3g, Fats: 16.9g

Lunch:

½ cup brown rice, cooked
1 medium-sized carrot, cooked
¼ cup spring onions, fresh
Nutritional values: Kcal: 377 Protein: 8.1g, Carbs: 80.2g, Dietary Fiber: 5.4g, Fats: 2.6g

Snack:

2 Graham crackers
4 medium-sized apricots
10 oz raspberries
Nutritional values: Kcal: 333 Protein: 7.1g, Carbs: 70.7g, Dietary Fiber: 21.9g, Fats: 5.6g

Dinner:

3.5 oz green peas
7 oz spinach, stewed
1 oz almonds, toasted
2 tbsp olive oil
Nutritional values: Kcal: 530 Protein: 17.1g, Carbs: 27.6g, Dietary Fiber: 13g, Fats: 43.4g

Day 59

Breakfast

1 cup of blueberries, fresh
¼ cup of blackberries, fresh
5 walnuts
1 cup of herbal tea
Nutritional values: Kcal: 274 Protein: 8.3g, Carbs: 27.7g, Dietary Fiber: 7.3g, Fats: 17.2g

Snack:

1 cup edamame hummus
½ cup beets, cooked
½ cup shallots, fresh
Nutritional values: Kcal: 471 Protein: 36.6g, Carbs: 50.2g, Dietary Fiber: 12.4g, Fats: 17.6g

Lunch:

7 oz red bell peppers, grilled
1 tbsp olive oil
7 oz lettuce
1 cup freshly squeezed orange juice
Nutritional values: Kcal: 525 Protein: 11g, Carbs: 94.8g, Dietary Fiber: 13g, Fats: 17g

Snack:

1 medium-sized grapefruit
1 oz walnuts
Nutritional values: Kcal: 216 Protein: 7.6g, Carbs: 13.2g, Dietary Fiber: 3.3g, Fats: 16.9g

Dinner:

1 large zucchini, grilled and seasoned with 1 tbsp olive oil
2 slices buckwheat bread
1 pear
Nutritional values: Kcal: 403 Protein: 8.7g, Carbs: 60.7g, Dietary Fiber: 9.2g, Fats: 16.6g

Day 60

Breakfast:

1 cup of blueberries, fresh
¼ cup of blackberries, fresh
5 walnuts
1 cup of herbal tea
Nutritional values: Kcal: 274 Protein: 8.3g, Carbs: 27.7g, Dietary Fiber: 7.3g, Fats: 17.2g

Snack:

1 banana
1 oz pecan nuts
Nutritional values: Kcal: 302 Protein: 4.3g, Carbs: 31g, Dietary Fiber: 6.1g, Fats: 20.6g

Lunch:

1 medium-sized zucchini, grilled
2 large red bell peppers, grilled
1 tbsp olive oil
¼ cup basmati rice
1 fig
Nutritional values: Kcal: 405 Protein: 7.5g, Carbs: 64.7g, Dietary Fiber: 6.2g, Fats: 15.1g

Snack:

4 large oranges, juiced
Nutritional values: Kcal: 272 Protein: 6.9g, Carbs: 86.4g, Dietary Fiber: 17.6g, Fats: 0.8g

Dinner:

5 oz eggplant, steamed
½ cup red lentils, cooked
2 cherry tomatoes, fresh
Nutritional values: Kcal: 419 Protein: 28.3g, Carbs: 75.6g, Dietary Fiber: 37.2g, Fats: 1.8g

Day 61
Breakfast:
½ cup rolled oats
1 tbsp flaxseed
½ cup coconut milk
Nutritional values: Kcal: 468 Protein: 9.4g, Carbs: 36.4g, Dietary Fiber: 8.7g, Fats: 33.5g
Snack:
1 oz pecans
1 large orange
Nutritional values: Kcal: 284 Protein: 4.8g, Carbs: 25.7g, Dietary Fiber: 7.5g, Fats: 4.8g
Lunch:
1 large zucchini, grilled and seasoned with 1 tbsp olive oil
2 slices buckwheat bread
1 pear
Nutritional values: Kcal: 403 Protein: 8.7g, Carbs: 60.7g, Dietary Fiber: 9.2g, Fats: 16.6g
Snack:
3 cups pineapple chunks, juiced
1 large apple, juiced
Nutritional values: Kcal: 315 Protein: 3.5g, Carbs: 92g, Dietary Fiber: 12.7g, Fats: 0.9g
Dinner
10 oz mushrooms, grilled
½ cup basmati rice, cooked
Nutritional values: Kcal: 398 Protein: 15.5g, Carbs: 83.3g, Dietary Fiber: 4g, Fats: 1.4g

Day 62
Breakfast:
1 cup almond yogurt
1 tbsp chia seeds
3 figs
1 cup of black coffee
Nutritional values: Kcal: 457 Protein: 22.1g, Carbs: 64.2g, Dietary Fiber: 16g, Fats: 13.1g
Snack:
½ avocado, grilled
3 plums
Nutritional values: Kcal: 295 Protein: 3.4g, Carbs: 32.6g, Dietary Fiber: 9.4g, Fats: 20.2g
Lunch:
1 cup green peas, cooked
½ cup hummus
7 oz mushrooms, grilled
1.5 oz cauliflower, grilled
Nutritional values: Kcal: 392 Protein: 25.9g, Carbs: 50.6g, Dietary Fiber: 19.4g, Fats: 13.2g
Snack:
1 large apple
2 medium-sized carrots
2 oz prunes
Nutritional values: Kcal: 302 Protein: 2.8g, Carbs: 79g, Dietary Fiber: 12.4g, Fats: 0.6g
Dinner:
7 oz buckwheat noodles, cooked and seasoned with one tablespoon of olive oil
2 oz spring onions, steamed
Nutritional values: Kcal: 412 Protein: 10.1g, Carbs: 54.1g, Dietary Fiber: 3.8g, Fats: 18.2g

Day 63

Breakfast:

10 oz tomatoes, grilled
7 oz asparagus, grilled
1 cup of freshly squeezed orange juice
4 large figs
Nutritional values: Kcal: 392 Protein: 11.1g,
Carbs: 93.1g, Dietary Fiber: 15.5g, Fats: 2g

Snack:

1 cup grapes
1 large mango
2 kiwis
Nutritional values: Kcal: 355 Protein: 5.1g, Carbs:
88.1g, Dietary Fiber: 10.4g, Fats: 2.4g

Lunch:

7 oz artichoke
½ cup kidney beans
1 tbsp extra virgin olive oil
Nutritional values: Kcal: 523 Protein: 27.2g,
Carbs: 77.2g, Dietary Fiber: 24.7g, Fats: 15.3g

Snack:

1 large apple
Nutritional values: Kcal: 116 Protein: 0.6g, Carbs:
30.8g, Dietary Fiber: 5.4g, Fats: 0.4g

Dinner:

7 oz arugula
1 cup raspberries
1 oz walnuts
1 cup freshly squeezed orange juice
Nutritional values: Kcal: 401 Protein: 15.1g,
Carbs: 50.5g, Dietary Fiber: 13.6g, Fats: 19.3g

Day 64
Breakfast:
2 bananas
1 tbsp pure coconut nectar
1 tbsp flaxseed
1 cup freshly squeezed lemonade
Nutritional values: Kcal: 369 Protein: 5.9g, Carbs: 78.3g, Dietary Fiber: 9.1g, Fats: 4.9g
Snack:
½ cup blueberries
1 oz almonds, toasted
1 oz walnuts
Nutritional values: Kcal: 381 Protein: 13.4g, Carbs: 19.4g, Dietary Fiber: 7.2g, Fats: 31.2g
Lunch:
3 oz red lentils, cooked
1 carrot cooked
7 oz kale, steamed
2 oz lettuce
Nutritional values: Kcal: 435 Protein: 28.7g, Carbs: 80.6g, Dietary Fiber: 31g, Fats: 1g
Snack:
3 cups honeydew melon, juiced
1 cup watermelon, diced
Nutritional values: Kcal: 203 Protein: 3.5g, Carbs: 55g, Dietary Fiber: 4.5g, Fats: 0.9g
Dinner:
5 oz eggplant, steamed
½ cup red lentils, cooked
2 cherry tomatoes, fresh
Nutritional values: Kcal: 419 Protein: 28.3g, Carbs: 75.6g, Dietary Fiber: 37.2g, Fats: 1.8g

Day 65:
Breakfast:
½ cup quinoa, cooked
3 tbsp raisins
¼ cup coconut milk
1 cup of black coffee
Nutritional values: Kcal: 532 Protein: 14.2g,
Carbs: 79.4g, Dietary Fiber: 8.3g, Fats: 19.6g
Snack:
1 oz pecan nuts
Nutritional values: Kcal: 197 Protein: 3g, Carbs:
4g, Dietary Fiber: 3g, Fats: 20.2g
Lunch:
2 medium-sized corn tortillas
¼ cup black beans, cooked
1 large tomato, diced
7 oz of spinach, steamed
1 red bell pepper
Nutritional values: Kcal: 386 Protein: 21.7g,
Carbs: 75g, Dietary Fiber: 18.5g, Fats: 3.5g
Snack:
1 cup cantaloupe
6 dates
Nutritional values: Kcal: 193 Protein: 2.5g, Carbs:
50.1g, Dietary Fiber: 5.4g, Fats: 0.5g
Dinner:
1 cup edamame hummus
½ cup beets, cooked
½ cup shallots, fresh
Nutritional values: Kcal: 471 Protein: 36.6g,
Carbs: 50.2g, Dietary Fiber: 12.4g, Fats: 17.6g

Day 66:
Breakfast:
1 cup of strawberries, fresh
½ cup raspberries, fresh
5 almonds, toasted
½ cup almond yogurt
1 cup of herbal tea
Nutritional values: Kcal: 200 Protein: 10g, Carbs: 28.3g, Dietary Fiber: 7.6g, Fats: 5.3g
Snack:
1 peach
2 oz pecan nuts
Nutritional values: Kcal: 454 Protein: 7.5g, Carbs: 22.1g, Dietary Fiber: 8.4g, Fats: 40.9g
Lunch:
4 Roma tomatoes, grilled
½ cup rice, cooked
½ spinach, steamed
Nutritional values: Kcal: 436 Protein: 11.9g, Carbs: 92g, Dietary Fiber: 9.5g, Fats: 3.6g
Snack:
1 red bell pepper
1 yellow bell pepper
1 green bell pepper
1 cup avocado chunks
Nutritional values: Kcal: 412 Protein: 6.4g, Carbs: 39.6g, Dietary Fiber: 14.6g, Fats: 29.4g
Dinner:
3.5 oz buckwheat pasta, cooked
1 large tomato
3.5 oz lettuce
Nutritional values: Kcal: 330 Protein: 13.2g, Carbs: 63.9g, Dietary Fiber: 2.7g, Fats: 2.8g

Day 67:
Breakfast:
2 large oranges, broiled
2 oz walnuts
1 cup of herbal tea
Nutritional values: Kcal: 523 Protein: 17.1g,
Carbs: 48.9g, Dietary Fiber: 12.7g, Fats: 33.9g
Snack:
4 medium-sized oranges, juiced
Nutritional values: Kcal: 200 Protein: 4.9g, Carbs:
64.5g, Dietary Fiber: 12.4g, Fats: 0.6g
Lunch:
2 cup butternut squash, cooked
1 cup Brussel sprouts, cooked
1 cup leeks, cooked
1 tbsp olive oil
Nutritional values: Kcal: 338 Protein: 71g, Carbs:
53.3g, Dietary Fiber: 10.5g, Fats: 14.8g
Snack:
7 oz chestnuts, baked
Nutritional values: Kcal: 389 Protein: 3.2g, Carbs:
87.7g, Dietary Fiber: 8.7g, Fats: 2.5g
Dinner:
5 oz orzo pasta, cooked
½ cup zucchini, grilled
Nutritional values: Kcal: 417 Protein: 16.7g,
Carbs: 79.5g, Dietary Fiber: 0.6g, Fats: 3.4g

Day 68:
Breakfast:
10 oz grilled red peppers
10 oz melon
4 pecans
1 cup of herbal tea
Nutritional values: Kcal: 212 Protein: 7.7g, Carbs: 48.6g, Dietary Fiber: 6.8g, Fats: 1.8g
Snack:
1 oz pecan nuts
Nutritional values: Kcal: 395 Protein: 6.1g, Carbs: 8.1g, Dietary Fiber: 6.1g, Fats: 40.5g
Lunch:
5 oz mushrooms, grilled
1 white onion, grilled
1 tbsp olive oil
Nutritional values: Kcal: 241 Protein: 3.4g, Carbs: 29.8g, Dietary Fiber: 5.3g, Fats: 14.4g
Snack:
7 oz avocado, baked
Nutritional values: Kcal: 405 Protein: 3.8g, Carbs: 17.1g, Dietary Fiber: 13.3g, Fats: 38.7g
Dinner:
1 tomato, fire-roasted
1 zucchini, grilled
7 oz turnip greens, fresh
1 oz walnuts
1 cup freshly squeezed orange juice
Nutritional values: Kcal: 393 Protein: 14.4g, Carbs: 51.7g, Dietary Fiber: 11.7g, Fats: 18.3g

Day 69:
Breakfast:
10 oz grilled red peppers
2 oz quinoa, cooked
10 oz melon
4 pecans
1 cup of herbal tea
Nutritional values: Kcal: 421 Protein: 15.7g,
Carbs: 85g, Dietary Fiber: 10.8g, Fats: 5.2g
Snack:
1 kiwi
1.5 oz almonds, toasted
Nutritional values: Kcal: 292 Protein: 9.9g, Carbs:
20.2g, Dietary Fiber: 7.6g, Fats: 21.7g
Lunch:
5 oz arugula, fresh
½ cup white beans, cooked
1 red onion, fresh
Nutritional values: Kcal: 416 Protein: 28.5g,
Carbs: 76.3g, Dietary Fiber: 20g, Fats: 1.9g
Snack:
1 medium apple
1 banana
Nutritional values: Kcal: 221 Protein: 1.9g, Carbs:
57.8g, Dietary Fiber: 8.5g, Fats: 0.8g
Dinner:
3.5 oz buckwheat noodles, cooked and seasoned
with one tablespoon of olive oil
2 oz spring onions, steamed
3.5 oz kale, steamed
Nutritional values: Kcal: 512 Protein: 16.1g,
Carbs: 83.1g, Dietary Fiber: 12.7g, Fats: 17.2g

Day 70
Breakfast:
¼ cup rolled oats
¼ cup almond milk
5 oz cherries
Nutritional values: Kcal: 379 Protein: 4.6g, Carbs: 56.8g, Dietary Fiber: 4.2g, Fats: 15.7g
Snack:
2 peaches
1 oz walnuts
Nutritional values: Kcal: 293 Protein: 9.6g, Carbs: 30.8g, Dietary Fiber: 6.5g, Fats: 17.5g
Lunch:
7 oz hummus
1 oz buckwheat bread
7 oz carrot sticks
Nutritional values: Kcal: 486 Protein: 19.5g, Carbs: 62.2g, Dietary Fiber: 17.5g, Fats: 20g
Snack:
3.5 oz cherries
Nutritional values: Kcal: 114 Protein: 0.4g, Carbs: 27.8g, Dietary Fiber: 0.6g, Fats: 0.1g
Dinner:
7 oz sweet potato, baked
¼ cup kidney beans, cooked
1 oz buckwheat bread
1 cup of herbal tea
Nutritional values: Kcal: 410 Protein: 16.5g, Carbs: 83.6g, Dietary Fiber: 14.3g, Fats: 1.8g

Day 71

Breakfast:

¼ cup rolled oats

¼ cup almond milk

1 oz brazil nuts

Nutritional values: Kcal: 401 Protein: 8.2g, Carbs: 20.6g, Dietary Fiber: 5.5g, Fats: 34.6g

Snack:

1 medium-sized mango

4 medium-sized plums

Nutritional values: Kcal: 321 Protein: 4.8g, Carbs: 82g, Dietary Fiber: 8.6g, Fats: 2.1g

Lunch:

3.5 oz green peas

7 oz spinach, stewed

1 oz almonds, toasted

2 tbsp olive oil

Nutritional values: Kcal: 530 Protein: 17.1g, Carbs: 27.6g, Dietary Fiber: 13g, Fats: 43.4g

Snack:

1 cup of freshly squeezed orange juice

Nutritional values: Kcal: 112 Protein: 1.7g, Carbs: 25.8g, Dietary Fiber: 0.5g, Fats: 0.5g

Dinner:

7 oz spinach, steamed

1 red onion, fresh

2 oz pine nuts

Nutritional values: Kcal: 471 Protein: 14.6g, Carbs: 24.9g, Dietary Fiber: 8.8g, Fats: 39.7g

Day 72

Breakfast

1 large apple, baked
1 cup of raspberries, fresh
1 cup of freshly squeezed orange juice
Nutritional values: Kcal: 292 Protein: 3.8g, Carbs: 71.3g, Dietary Fiber: 13.9g, Fats: 1.7g

Snack:

1 oz pecan nuts
Nutritional values: Kcal: 395 Protein: 6.1g, Carbs: 8.1g, Dietary Fiber: 6.1g, Fats: 40.5g

Lunch:

½ cup leek, cooked
1 medium-sized potato, cooked
½ cup shallots, cooked
1 tbsp olive oil
Nutritional values: Kcal: 369 Protein: 7g, Carbs: 56.9g, Dietary Fiber: 5.5g, Fats: 14.4g

Snack:

3.5 oz walnuts
Nutritional values: Kcal: 613 Protein: 23.9g, Carbs: 9.8g, Dietary Fiber: 6.8g, Fats: 58.5g

Dinner:

2 slices buckwheat bread
1 medium-sized tomato, fresh
1 small cucumber
1 red onion, fresh
1 tbsp olive oil
Nutritional values: Kcal: 268 Protein: 5.1g, Carbs: 32.7g, Dietary Fiber: 5g, Fats: 15.1g

Day 73

Breakfast
1 cup almond yogurt
7 oz pineapple chunks
1 large orange
1 cup of herbal tea
Nutritional values: Kcal: 362 Protein: 16.8g,
Carbs: 65.4g, Dietary Fiber: 7.2g, Fats: 3.5g
Snack:
7 oz cherries
Nutritional values: Kcal: 228 Protein: 0.7g, Carbs:
55.6g, Dietary Fiber: 1.2g, Fats: 0.1g
Lunch:
½ cup barley, cooked
¼ cup red lentils, cooked
2 medium-sized tomatoes, fire-roasted
Nutritional values: Kcal: 539 Protein: 26g, Carbs:
106g, Dietary Fiber: 33.5g, Fats: 3.1g
Snack:
1 cup of freshly squeezed lemon juice
1.5 oz walnuts
Nutritional values: Kcal: 321 Protein: 12.2g,
Carbs: 9.3g, Dietary Fiber: 3.9g, Fats: 27g
Dinner:
7 oz artichoke, grilled
1 cup yellow wax beans, cooked
2 tbsp olive oil
2 oz lettuce
Nutritional values: Kcal: 375 Protein: 8.8g, Carbs:
30.4g, Dietary Fiber: 14.8g, Fats: 28.5g

Day 74

Breakfast:
1 cup strawberries, fresh
¼ cup almond milk
1 medium-sized apple
1 oz walnuts
Nutritional values: Kcal: 348 Protein: 4.8g, Carbs: 46g, Dietary Fiber: 10.1g, Fats: 19.7g
Snack:
10 oz honeydew melon, fresh
10 oz cherries, fresh
Nutritional values: Kcal: 428 Protein: 2.6g, Carbs: 105.1g, Dietary Fiber: 4g, Fats: 0.6g
Lunch:
3.5 oz buckwheat pasta, cooked
1 large tomato
3.5 oz lettuce
Nutritional values: Kcal: 330 Protein: 13.2g, Carbs: 63.9g, Dietary Fiber: 2.7g, Fats: 2.8g
Snack:
10 oz grapefruit
1 medium-sized kiwi
1 oz walnuts
Nutritional values: Kcal: 312 Protein: 9.5g, Carbs: 36.9g, Dietary Fiber: 7.3g, Fats: 17.4g
Dinner:
7 oz buckwheat noodles, cooked and seasoned with one tablespoon of olive oil
2 oz spring onions, steamed
Nutritional values: Kcal: 412 Protein: 10.1g, Carbs: 54.1g, Dietary Fiber: 3.8g, Fats: 18.2g

Day 75

Breakfast:
1 cup almond yogurt
1 tbsp chia seeds
3 figs
1 cup of black coffee
Nutritional values: Kcal: 457 Protein: 22.1g,
Carbs: 64.2g, Dietary Fiber: 16g, Fats: 13.1g
Snack:
4 cups blueberries, juiced
Nutritional values: Kcal: 280 Protein: 1.96g,
Carbs: 85.8g, Dietary Fiber: 14.4g, Fats: 1.9g
Lunch:
7 oz artichoke
½ cup kidney beans
1 tbsp extra virgin olive oil
Nutritional values: Kcal: 523 Protein: 27.2g,
Carbs: 77.2g, Dietary Fiber: 24.7g, Fats: 15.3g
Snack:
1 avocado, juiced
Nutritional values: Kcal: 268 Protein: 4g, Carbs:
17.1g, Dietary Fiber: 13.5g, Fats: 29.4g
Dinner:
7 oz arugula
1 cup raspberries
1 oz walnuts
1 cup freshly squeezed orange juice
Nutritional values: Kcal: 401 Protein: 15.1g,
Carbs: 50.5g, Dietary Fiber: 13.6g, Fats: 19.3g

Day 76
Breakfast:
2 bananas
1 tbsp pure coconut nectar
1 tbsp flaxseed
1 cup freshly squeezed lemonade
Nutritional values: Kcal: 369 Protein: 5.9g, Carbs: 78.3g, Dietary Fiber: 9.1g, Fats: 4.9g
Snack:
1 cup of freshly squeezed lemon juice
1.5 oz walnuts
Nutritional values: Kcal: 321 Protein: 12.2g, Carbs: 9.3g, Dietary Fiber: 3.9g, Fats: 27g
Lunch:
5 oz eggplant, steamed
½ cup red lentils, cooked
2 cherry tomatoes, fresh
Nutritional values: Kcal: 419 Protein: 28.3g, Carbs: 75.6g, Dietary Fiber: 37.2g, Fats: 1.8g
Snack:
7 oz grapes
1 oz pecan nuts
Nutritional values: Kcal: 330 Protein: 4.3g, Carbs: 38.1g, Dietary Fiber: 4.8g, Fats: 20.9g
Dinner:
3 oz red lentils, cooked
1 carrot cooked
7 oz kale, steamed
2 oz lettuce
Nutritional values: Kcal: 435 Protein: 28.7g, Carbs: 80.6g, Dietary Fiber: 31g, Fats: 1g

Day 77
Breakfast:
½ cup quinoa, cooked
3 tbsp raisins
¼ cup coconut milk
1 cup of black coffee
Nutritional values: Kcal: 532 Protein: 14.2g,
Carbs: 79.4g, Dietary Fiber: 8.3g, Fats: 19.6g
Snack:
1 cup cantaloupe, fresh
6 dates
Nutritional values: Kcal: 193 Protein: 2.5g, Carbs:
50.1g, Dietary Fiber: 5.4g, Fats: 0.5g
Lunch:
10oz shiitake mushrooms, grilled
4 oz leeks, stewed
3.5 oz radicchio, fresh
1 oz walnuts
Nutritional values: Kcal 420: Protein: 14.3g,
Carbs: 62.4g, Dietary Fiber: 10.8g, Fats: 18g
Snack:
4 medium-sized apricots
10 oz raspberries
Nutritional values: Kcal: 214 Protein: 5.2g, Carbs:
49.2g, Dietary Fiber: 21.1g, Fats: 2.7g
Dinner:
4 Roma tomatoes, grilled
½ cup rice, cooked
½ spinach, steamed
Nutritional values: Kcal: 436 Protein: 11.9g,
Carbs: 92g, Dietary Fiber: 9.5g, Fats: 3.6g

Day 78
Breakfast:
2 large oranges, broiled
2 oz walnuts
1 cup of herbal tea
Nutritional values: Kcal: 523 Protein: 17.1g,
Carbs: 48.9g, Dietary Fiber: 12.7g, Fats: 33.9g
Snack:
1 avocado, juiced
Nutritional values: Kcal: 268 Protein: 4g, Carbs:
17.1g, Dietary Fiber: 13.5g, Fats: 29.4g
Lunch:
3.5 oz green peas
7 oz spinach, stewed
1 oz almonds, toasted
2 tbsp olive oil
Nutritional values: Kcal: 530 Protein: 17.1g,
Carbs: 27.6g, Dietary Fiber: 13g, Fats: 43.4g
Snack:
1 medium-sized orange
Nutritional values: Kcal: 86 Protein: 1.7g, Carbs:
21.6g, Dietary Fiber: 4.4g, Fats: 0.2g
Dinner:
½ cup brown rice, cooked
1 medium-sized carrot, cooked
¼ cup spring onions, fresh
Nutritional values: Kcal: 377 Protein: 8.1g, Carbs:
80.2g, Dietary Fiber: 5.4g, Fats: 2.6g

Day 79
Breakfast:
1 large apple, baked
1 cup of raspberries, fresh
1 oz pecan nuts
Nutritional values: Kcal: 377 Protein: 5.1g, Carbs: 49.5g, Dietary Fiber: 16.4g, Fats: 21.4g
Snack:
2 Graham crackers
4 medium-sized apricots
10 oz raspberries
Nutritional values: Kcal: 333 Protein: 7.1g, Carbs: 70.7g, Dietary Fiber: 21.9g, Fats: 5.6g
Lunch:
1 medium-sized zucchini, grilled
2 large red bell peppers, grilled
1 tbsp olive oil
¼ cup basmati rice
1 fig
Nutritional values: Kcal: 405 Protein: 7.5g, Carbs: 64.7g, Dietary Fiber: 6.2g, Fats: 15.1g
Snack:
½ medium-sized avocado
1 medium-sized tomato, fresh
2 slices buckwheat bread
1 large orange, juiced
Nutritional values: Kcal: 351 Protein: 5.6g, Carbs: 41.8g, Dietary Fiber: 12.3g, Fats: 25g
Dinner
7 oz red bell peppers, grilled
1 tbsp olive oil
7 oz lettuce
1 cup freshly squeezed orange juice
Nutritional values: Kcal: 525 Protein: 11g, Carbs: 94.8g, Dietary Fiber: 13g, Fats: 17g

Day 80
Breakfast:
5 large strawberries
1 medium-sized apple
1 oz pecan nuts
1 cup of freshly squeezed orange juice
Nutritional values: Kcal: 454 Protein: 5.9g, Carbs: 67.6g, Dietary Fiber: 10.7g, Fats: 21.4g
Snack:
4 large oranges, juiced
Nutritional values: Kcal: 272 Protein: 6.9g, Carbs: 86.4g, Dietary Fiber: 17.6g, Fats: 0.8g
Lunch:
2 oz quinoa, cooked
2 oz white beans, cooked
7 oz spinach, sautéed
1 pear
Nutritional values: Kcal: 524 Protein: 27.4g, Carbs: 98.9g, Dietary Fiber: 21.3g, Fats: 4.9g
Snack:
3.5 oz cherries
Nutritional values: Kcal: 114 Protein: 0.4g, Carbs: 27.8g, Dietary Fiber: 0.6g, Fats: 0.1g
Dinner:
10 oz button mushrooms, grilled
4 oz leeks, stewed
3.5 oz radicchio, fresh
1 oz walnuts
Nutritional values: Kcal 420: Protein: 14.3g, Carbs: 62.4g, Dietary Fiber: 10.8g, Fats: 18g

Day 81
Breakfast:
1 cup of blueberries, fresh
¼ cup of blackberries, fresh
5 walnuts
1 cup of herbal tea
Nutritional values: Kcal: 274 Protein: 8.3g, Carbs: 27.7g, Dietary Fiber: 7.3g, Fats: 17.2g
Snack:
7 oz avocado, baked
Nutritional values: Kcal: 405 Protein: 3.8g, Carbs: 17.1g, Dietary Fiber: 13.3g, Fats: 38.7g
Lunch:
5 oz arugula, fresh
½ cup white beans, cooked
1 red onion, fresh
Nutritional values: Kcal: 416 Protein: 28.5g, Carbs: 76.3g, Dietary Fiber: 20g, Fats: 1.9g
Snack:
2 peaches
1 oz walnuts
Nutritional values: Kcal: 293 Protein: 9.6g, Carbs: 30.8g, Dietary Fiber: 6.5g, Fats: 17.5g
Dinner:
7 oz sweet potato, baked
¼ cup kidney beans, cooked
1 oz buckwheat bread
1 cup of herbal tea
Nutritional values: Kcal: 410 Protein: 16.5g, Carbs: 83.6g, Dietary Fiber: 14.3g, Fats: 1.8g

Day 82

Breakfast:

1 banana

4 oz cherries

1 buckwheat wrap

Nutritional values: Kcal: 406 Protein: 5.5g, Carbs: 88.9g, Dietary Fiber: 5g, Fats: 3.6g

Snack:

4 oz strawberries

4 Graham crackers

1 large orange, juiced

Nutritional values: Kcal: 360 Protein: 6.3g, Carbs: 73.3g, Dietary Fiber: 8.3g, Fats: 6.2g

Lunch:

½ cup button mushrooms, grilled

1 cup celery, fresh

½ cup black beans, cooked

1 peach

Nutritional values: Kcal: 413 Protein: 24.1g, Carbs: 78.6g, Dietary Fiber: 19g, Fats: 2g

Snack:

½ cup blueberries

1 oz almonds, toasted

1 oz walnuts

Nutritional values: Kcal: 381 Protein: 13.4g, Carbs: 19.4g, Dietary Fiber: 7.2g, Fats: 31.2g

Dinner:

½ small eggplant, grilled

½ cup kidney beans, cooked

2 oz raspberries

Nutritional values: Kcal: 397 Protein: 23.6g, Carbs: 76.6g, Dietary Fiber: 25.8g, Fats: 1.8g

Day 83

Breakfast:

1 banana

1 oz pecan nuts

Nutritional values: Kcal: 302 Protein: 4.3g, Carbs: 31g, Dietary Fiber: 6.1g, Fats: 20.6g

Snack:

2 oz almonds, toasted

1 medium-sized apple

Nutritional values: Kcal: 444 Protein: 12.6g, Carbs: 43g, Dietary Fiber: 12.5g, Fats: 28.8g

Lunch:

5 oz buckwheat noodles, cooked

2 oz tomato paste

1 small artichoke, steamed

4 dates

Nutritional values: Kcal: 396 Protein: 13.9g, Carbs: 84.7g, Dietary Fiber: 13.6g, Fats: 3.5g

Snack:

3.5 oz chestnuts, baked

1 medium-sized mango

Nutritional values: Kcal: 395 Protein: 4.4g, Carbs: 93.8g, Dietary Fiber: 5g, Fats: 2.5g

Dinner:

3 oz red lentils, cooked

1 carrot cooked

7 oz kale, steamed

2 oz lettuce

Nutritional values: Kcal: 435 Protein: 28.7g, Carbs: 80.6g, Dietary Fiber: 31g, Fats: 1g

Day 84
Breakfast:
1 cup of strawberries, fresh
½ cup raspberries, fresh
5 almonds, toasted
½ cup almond yogurt
1 cup of herbal tea
Nutritional values: Kcal: 200 Protein: 10g, Carbs: 28.3g, Dietary Fiber: 7.6g, Fats: 5.3g
Snack:
10 oz avocado, baked
1 cup of herbal tea
Nutritional values: Kcal: 578 Protein: 5.4g, Carbs: 24.4g, Dietary Fiber: 19g, Fats: 55.3g
Lunch:
½ cup brown rice, cooked
1 medium-sized carrot, cooked
¼ cup spring onions, fresh
Nutritional values: Kcal: 377 Protein: 8.1g, Carbs: 80.2g, Dietary Fiber: 5.4g, Fats: 2.6g
Snack:
1 medium-sized mango
4 medium-sized plums
Nutritional values: Kcal: 321 Protein: 4.8g, Carbs: 82g, Dietary Fiber: 8.6g, Fats: 2.1g
Dinner:
7 oz buckwheat noodles, cooked and seasoned with one tablespoon of olive oil
2 oz spring onions, steamed
Nutritional values: Kcal: 412 Protein: 10.1g, Carbs: 54.1g, Dietary Fiber: 3.8g, Fats: 18.2g

Day 85

Breakfast:

1 large baked apple
1 cup of freshly squeezed orange juice
Nutritional values: Kcal: 228 Protein: 2.3g, Carbs: 56.6g, Dietary Fiber: 5.9g, Fats: 0.9g

Snack:

3.5 oz walnuts
Nutritional values: Kcal: 613 Protein: 23.9g, Carbs: 9.8g, Dietary Fiber: 6.8g, Fats: 58.5g

Lunch:

5 oz shiitake mushrooms, grilled
1 white onion, grilled
1 tbsp olive oil
Nutritional values: Kcal: 241 Protein: 3.4g, Carbs: 29.8g, Dietary Fiber: 5.3g, Fats: 14.4g

Snack:

1 medium-sized grapefruit
1 oz walnuts
Nutritional values: Kcal: 257 Protein: 8.4g, Carbs: 23.5g, Dietary Fiber: 4.8g, Fats: 17g

Dinner:

7 oz sweet potato, baked
¼ cup kidney beans, cooked
1 oz buckwheat bread
1 cup of herbal tea
Nutritional values: Kcal: 410 Protein: 16.5g, Carbs: 83.6g, Dietary Fiber: 14.3g, Fats: 1.8g

Day 86

Breakfast:

2 bananas

1 tbsp pure coconut nectar

1 tbsp flaxseed

1 cup freshly squeezed lemonade

Nutritional values: Kcal: 369 Protein: 5.9g, Carbs: 78.3g, Dietary Fiber: 9.1g, Fats: 4.9g

Snack:

1 banana

1 oz pecan nuts

Nutritional values: Kcal: 302 Protein: 4.3g, Carbs: 31g, Dietary Fiber: 6.1g, Fats: 20.6g

Lunch:

1 cup edamame hummus

½ cup beets, cooked

½ cup shallots, fresh

Nutritional values: Kcal: 471 Protein: 36.6g, Carbs: 50.2g, Dietary Fiber: 12.4g, Fats: 17.6g

Snack:

7 oz chestnuts, baked

Nutritional values: Kcal: 389 Protein: 3.2g, Carbs: 87.7g, Dietary Fiber: 8.7g, Fats: 2.5g

Dinner:

1 tomato, fire-roasted

1 zucchini, grilled

7 oz turnip greens, fresh

1 oz walnuts

1 cup freshly squeezed orange juice

Nutritional values: Kcal: 393 Protein: 14.4g, Carbs: 51.7g, Dietary Fiber: 11.7g, Fats: 18.3g

Day 87

Breakfast:

1 large baked apple
1 cup of freshly squeezed orange juice
Nutritional values: Kcal: 228 Protein: 2.3g, Carbs: 56.6g, Dietary Fiber: 5.9g, Fats: 0.9g

Snack:

1 red bell pepper
1 yellow bell pepper
1 green bell pepper
1 cup avocado chunks
Nutritional values: Kcal: 412 Protein: 6.4g, Carbs: 39.6g, Dietary Fiber: 14.6g, Fats: 29.4g

Lunch:

2 cup butternut squash, cooked
1 cup brussel sprouts, cooked
1 cup leeks, cooked
1 tbsp olive oil
Nutritional values: Kcal: 338 Protein: 71g, Carbs: 53.3g, Dietary Fiber: 10.5g, Fats: 14.8g

Snack:

1 oz pecan nuts
Nutritional values: Kcal: 395 Protein: 6.1g, Carbs: 8.1g, Dietary Fiber: 6.1g, Fats: 40.5g

Dinner:

5 oz arugula, fresh
½ cup white beans, cooked
1 red onion, fresh
Nutritional values: Kcal: 416 Protein: 28.5g, Carbs: 76.3g, Dietary Fiber: 20g, Fats: 1.9g

Day 88
Breakfast:
2 apples, baked
1 cup of herbal tea
Nutritional values: Kcal: 234 Protein: 1.2g, Carbs: 62.1g, Dietary Fiber: 10.8g, Fats: 0.8g
Snack:
7 oz avocado, baked
Nutritional values: Kcal: 405 Protein: 3.8g, Carbs: 17.1g, Dietary Fiber: 13.3g, Fats: 38.7g
Lunch:
7 oz hummus
1 oz buckwheat bread
7 oz carrot sticks
Nutritional values: Kcal: 486 Protein: 19.5g, Carbs: 62.2g, Dietary Fiber: 17.5g, Fats: 20g
Snack:
1 medium-sized mango
4 medium-sized plums
Nutritional values: Kcal: 321 Protein: 4.8g, Carbs: 82g, Dietary Fiber: 8.6g, Fats: 2.1g
Dinner:
1 cup button mushrooms, grilled
2 large carrots, grilled
1 medium-sized potato, cooked and mashed
1 red bell pepper, grilled
1 tbsp olive oil
Nutritional values: Kcal: 396 Protein: 8.9g, Carbs: 62.7g, Dietary Fiber: 10.5g, Fats: 14.7g

Day 89

Breakfast:

1 large apple, baked
1 cup of raspberries, fresh
1 oz pecan nuts
Nutritional values: Kcal: 377 Protein: 5.1g, Carbs: 49.5g, Dietary Fiber: 16.4g, Fats: 21.4g

Snack:

1 avocado, juiced
Nutritional values: Kcal: 268 Protein: 4g, Carbs: 17.1g, Dietary Fiber: 13.5g, Fats: 29.4g

Lunch:

7 oz spinach, steamed
1 red onion, fresh
2 oz pine nuts
Nutritional values: Kcal: 471 Protein: 14.6g, Carbs: 24.9g, Dietary Fiber: 8.8g, Fats: 39.7g

Snack:

10 oz honeydew melon, fresh
10 oz cherries, fresh
Nutritional values: Kcal: 428 Protein: 2.6g, Carbs: 105.1g, Dietary Fiber: 4g, Fats: 0.6g

Dinner:

10 oz Portobello mushrooms, grilled
½ cup basmati rice, cooked
Nutritional values: Kcal: 398 Protein: 15.5g, Carbs: 83.3g, Dietary Fiber: 4g, Fats: 1.4g

Day 90
Breakfast:
1 large apple, baked
1 cup of raspberries, fresh
1 cup of freshly squeezed orange juice
Nutritional values: Kcal: 292 Protein: 3.8g, Carbs: 71.3g, Dietary Fiber: 13.9g, Fats: 1.7g
Snack:
1 peach
2 oz pecan nuts
Nutritional values: Kcal: 454 Protein: 7.5g, Carbs: 22.1g, Dietary Fiber: 8.4g, Fats: 40.9g
Lunch:
7 oz sweet potato, baked
¼ cup kidney beans, cooked
1 oz buckwheat bread
1 cup of herbal tea
Nutritional values: Kcal: 410 Protein: 16.5g, Carbs: 83.6g, Dietary Fiber: 14.3g, Fats: 1.8g
Snack:
1 kiwi
1.5 oz almonds, toasted
Nutritional values: Kcal: 292 Protein: 9.9g, Carbs: 20.2g, Dietary Fiber: 7.6g, Fats: 21.7g
Dinner:
10oz shiitake mushrooms, grilled
4 oz leeks, stewed
3.5 oz radicchio, fresh
1 oz walnuts
Nutritional values: Kcal 420: Protein: 14.3g, Carbs: 62.4g, Dietary Fiber: 10.8g, Fats: 18g

Day 91:

Breakfast

1 cup almond yogurt

7 oz pineapple chunks

1 large orange

1 cup of herbal tea

Nutritional values: Kcal: 362 Protein: 16.8g, Carbs: 65.4g, Dietary Fiber: 7.2g, Fats: 3.5g

Snack:

2 slices buckwheat bread

1 medium-sized tomato, fresh

1 small cucumber

1 red onion, fresh

1 tbsp olive oil

Nutritional values: Kcal: 268 Protein: 5.1g, Carbs: 32.7g, Dietary Fiber: 5g, Fats: 15.1g

Lunch:

3.5 oz enoki mushrooms, grilled

7 oz shiitake mushrooms, grilled

3.5 oz shishito peppers, grilled

2 oz buckwheat bread

Nutritional values: Kcal: 550 Protein: 20.6g, Carbs: 127g, Dietary Fiber: 34.3g, Fats: 5.8g

Snack:

7 oz cherries

Nutritional values: Kcal: 228 Protein: 0.7g, Carbs: 55.6g, Dietary Fiber: 1.2g, Fats: 0.1g

Dinner:

½ cup black beans, cooked

1 tbsp tahini

Nutritional values: Kcal: 420 Protein: 23.5g, Carbs: 63.7g, Dietary Fiber: 16.1g, Fats: 9.4g

Day 92:

Breakfast:

1 cup almond yogurt

1 tbsp chia seeds

3 figs

1 cup of black coffee

Nutritional values: Kcal: 457 Protein: 22.1g, Carbs: 64.2g, Dietary Fiber: 16g, Fats: 13.1g

Snack:

½ cup leek, cooked

1 medium-sized potato, cooked

½ cup shallots, cooked

1 tbsp olive oil

Nutritional values: Kcal: 369 Protein: 7g, Carbs: 56.9g, Dietary Fiber: 5.5g, Fats: 14.4g

Lunch:

1 cup edamame hummus

½ cup beets, cooked

½ cup shallots, fresh

Nutritional values: Kcal: 471 Protein: 36.6g, Carbs: 50.2g, Dietary Fiber: 12.4g, Fats: 17.6g

Snack:

1 cup of freshly squeezed lemon juice

1.5 oz walnuts

Nutritional values: Kcal: 321 Protein: 12.2g, Carbs: 9.3g, Dietary Fiber: 3.9g, Fats: 27g

Dinner:

10 oz mushrooms, grilled

½ cup basmati rice, cooked

Nutritional values: Kcal: 398 Protein: 15.5g, Carbs: 83.3g, Dietary Fiber: 4g, Fats: 1.4g

Day 93
Breakfast:
2 cups grapes
1 large orange
2 kiwis
1 cup lemonade
Nutritional values: Kcal: 319 Protein: 5.3g, Carbs: 80.9g, Dietary Fiber: 12.3g, Fats: 1.8g
Snack:
2 oz hazelnuts
Nutritional values: Kcal: 356 Protein: 8.5g, Carbs: 9.5g, Dietary Fiber: 5.5g, Fats: 34.5g
Lunch:
1 cup mushrooms, grilled
2 large carrots, grilled
1 medium-sized potato, cooked and mashed
1 red bell pepper, grilled
1 tbsp olive oil
Nutritional values: Kcal: 396 Protein: 8.9g, Carbs: 62.7g, Dietary Fiber: 10.5g, Fats: 14.7g
Snack:
2 medium apples
1 cup freshly squeezed orange juice
Nutritional values: Kcal: 344 Protein: 2.9g, Carbs: 87.4g, Dietary Fiber: 11.3g, Fats: 1.3g
Dinner:
3 oz red lentils, cooked
1 carrot cooked
7 oz kale, steamed
2 oz lettuce
Nutritional values: Kcal: 435 Protein: 28.7g, Carbs: 80.6g, Dietary Fiber: 31g, Fats: 1g

Day 94
Breakfast:
1 cup strawberries, fresh
¼ cup almond milk
1 medium apple
1 oz walnuts
Nutritional values: Kcal: 348 Protein: 4.8g, Carbs: 46g, Dietary Fiber: 10.1g, Fats: 19.7g
Snack:
4 large oranges, juiced
Nutritional values: Kcal: 272 Protein: 6.9g, Carbs: 86.4g, Dietary Fiber: 17.6g, Fats: 0.8g
Lunch:
½ cup barley, cooked
¼ cup red lentils, cooked
2 medium-sized tomatoes, fire-roasted
Nutritional values: Kcal: 539 Protein: 26g, Carbs: 106g, Dietary Fiber: 33.5g, Fats: 3.1g
Snack:
1 cup of freshly squeezed lemon juice
1.5 oz walnuts
Nutritional values: Kcal: 321 Protein: 12.2g, Carbs: 9.3g, Dietary Fiber: 3.9g, Fats: 27g
Dinner:
2 oz quinoa, cooked
2 oz white beans, cooked
7 oz spinach, sautéed
1 pear
Nutritional values: Kcal: 524 Protein: 27.4g, Carbs: 98.9g, Dietary Fiber: 21.3g, Fats: 4.9g

Day 95
Breakfast:
¼ cup rolled oats
¼ cup almond milk
1 oz brazil nuts
Nutritional values: Kcal: 401 Protein: 8.2g, Carbs: 20.6g, Dietary Fiber: 5.5g, Fats: 34.6g
Snack:
1 banana
1 oz pecan nuts
Nutritional values: Kcal: 302 Protein: 4.3g, Carbs: 31g, Dietary Fiber: 6.1g, Fats: 20.6g
Lunch:
7 oz artichoke, grilled
1 cup yellow wax beans, cooked
2 tbsp olive oil
2 oz lettuce
Nutritional values: Kcal: 375 Protein: 8.8g, Carbs: 30.4g, Dietary Fiber: 14.8g, Fats: 28.5g
Snack:
10 oz grapefruit
1 medium kiwi
1 oz walnuts
Nutritional values: Kcal: 312 Protein: 9.5g, Carbs: 36.9g, Dietary Fiber: 7.3g, Fats: 17.4g
Dinner:
½ cup green beans, cooked
1 medium-sized carrot, cooked
1 small sweet potato, cooked
½ cup broccoli, grilled
½ cup rice, cooked
Nutritional values: Kcal: 449 Protein: 10.6g, Carbs: 99.3g, Dietary Fiber: 7.8g, Fats: 0.9g

Day 96
Breakfast:
1 cup almond yogurt
2 oz prunes
1 tbsp flaxseed
1 tbsp pumpkin seeds
Nutritional values: Kcal: 394 Protein: 18.6g,
Carbs: 57g, Dietary Fiber: 6.3g, Fats: 9.4g
Snack:
3.5 oz chestnuts, baked
1 medium-sized mango
Nutritional values: Kcal: 395 Protein: 4.4g, Carbs:
93.8g, Dietary Fiber: 5g, Fats: 2.5g
Lunch:
7 oz red bell peppers, grilled
1 tbsp olive oil
7 oz lettuce
1 cup freshly squeezed orange juice
Nutritional values: Kcal: 525 Protein: 11g, Carbs:
94.8g, Dietary Fiber: 13g, Fats: 17g
Snack:
½ medium-sized avocado
1 medium-sized tomato, fresh
2 slices buckwheat bread
1 large orange, juiced
Nutritional values: Kcal: 351 Protein: 5.6g, Carbs:
41.8g, Dietary Fiber: 12.3g, Fats: 25g
Dinner:
3.5 oz chickpeas, cooked
3.5 oz lettuce
7 oz zucchini, grilled
Nutritional values: Kcal: 406 Protein: 22g, Carbs:
69.8g, Dietary Fiber: 20.1g, Fats: 6.5g

Day 97
Breakfast:
3 Wasa crackers
½ cup almond yogurt
1 tbsp chia seeds
7 oz pomegranate seeds
Nutritional values: Kcal: 385 Protein: 14.7g,
Carbs: 53.1g, Dietary Fiber: 11.8g, Fats: 11.1g
Snack:
4 cups blueberries, juiced
Nutritional values: Kcal: 280 Protein: 1.96g,
Carbs: 85.8g, Dietary Fiber: 14.4g, Fats: 1.9g
Lunch:
1 medium-sized zucchini, grilled
2 large red bell peppers, grilled
1 tbsp olive oil
¼ cup basmati rice
1 fig
Nutritional values: Kcal: 405 Protein: 7.5g, Carbs:
64.7g, Dietary Fiber: 6.2g, Fats: 15.1g
Snack:
½ cup strawberries, blended
½ cup blueberries, blended
4 Graham crackers
Nutritional values: Kcal: 301 Protein: 4.9g, Carbs:
59g, Dietary Fiber: 4.8g, Fats: 6.1g
Dinner:
7 oz spinach, steamed
1 red onion, fresh
2 oz pine nuts
Nutritional values: Kcal: 471 Protein: 14.6g,
Carbs: 24.9g, Dietary Fiber: 8.8g, Fats: 39.7g

Day 98
Breakfast
1 large apple, baked
1 cup of raspberries, fresh
1 oz pecan nuts
Nutritional values: Kcal: 377 Protein: 5.1g, Carbs: 49.5g, Dietary Fiber: 16.4g, Fats: 21.4g
Snack:
1 medium-sized grapefruit
1 oz walnuts
Nutritional values: Kcal: 216 Protein: 7.6g, Carbs: 13.2g, Dietary Fiber: 3.3g, Fats: 16.9g
Lunch:
½ cup brown rice, cooked
1 medium-sized carrot, cooked
¼ cup spring onions, fresh
Nutritional values: Kcal: 377 Protein: 8.1g, Carbs: 80.2g, Dietary Fiber: 5.4g, Fats: 2.6g
Snack:
2 Graham crackers
4 medium-sized apricots
10 oz raspberries
Nutritional values: Kcal: 333 Protein: 7.1g, Carbs: 70.7g, Dietary Fiber: 21.9g, Fats: 5.6g
Dinner:
3.5 oz green peas
7 oz spinach, stewed
1 oz almonds, toasted
2 tbsp olive oil
Nutritional values: Kcal: 530 Protein: 17.1g, Carbs: 27.6g, Dietary Fiber: 13g, Fats: 43.4g

Day 99
Breakfast
1 cup of blueberries, fresh
¼ cup of blackberries, fresh
5 walnuts
1 cup of herbal tea
Nutritional values: Kcal: 274 Protein: 8.3g, Carbs: 27.7g, Dietary Fiber: 7.3g, Fats: 17.2g
Snack:
1 cup edamame hummus
½ cup beets, cooked
½ cup shallots, fresh
Nutritional values: Kcal: 471 Protein: 36.6g, Carbs: 50.2g, Dietary Fiber: 12.4g, Fats: 17.6g
Lunch:
7 oz red bell peppers, grilled
1 tbsp olive oil
7 oz lettuce
1 cup freshly squeezed orange juice
Nutritional values: Kcal: 525 Protein: 11g, Carbs: 94.8g, Dietary Fiber: 13g, Fats: 17g
Snack:
1 medium-sized grapefruit
1 oz walnuts
Nutritional values: Kcal: 216 Protein: 7.6g, Carbs: 13.2g, Dietary Fiber: 3.3g, Fats: 16.9g
Dinner:
1 large zucchini, grilled and seasoned with 1 tbsp olive oil
2 slices buckwheat bread
1 pear
Nutritional values: Kcal: 403 Protein: 8.7g, Carbs: 60.7g, Dietary Fiber: 9.2g, Fats: 16.6g

Day 100
Breakfast:
1 cup of blueberries, fresh
¼ cup of blackberries, fresh
5 walnuts
1 cup of herbal tea
Nutritional values: Kcal: 274 Protein: 8.3g, Carbs: 27.7g, Dietary Fiber: 7.3g, Fats: 17.2g
Snack:
1 banana
1 oz pecan nuts
Nutritional values: Kcal: 302 Protein: 4.3g, Carbs: 31g, Dietary Fiber: 6.1g, Fats: 20.6g
Lunch:
1 medium-sized zucchini, grilled
2 large red bell peppers, grilled
1 tbsp olive oil
¼ cup basmati rice
1 fig
Nutritional values: Kcal: 405 Protein: 7.5g, Carbs: 64.7g, Dietary Fiber: 6.2g, Fats: 15.1g
Snack:
4 large oranges, juiced
Nutritional values: Kcal: 272 Protein: 6.9g, Carbs: 86.4g, Dietary Fiber: 17.6g, Fats: 0.8g
Dinner:
5 oz eggplant, steamed
½ cup red lentils, cooked
2 cherry tomatoes, fresh
Nutritional values: Kcal: 419 Protein: 28.3g, Carbs: 75.6g, Dietary Fiber: 37.2g, Fats: 1.8g

Chapter 3

Bodybuilding Tips

Here are some useful and positive tips to help you on your journey towards having the body and health you seek.

1. Preparing a weekly routine will help you be more efficient and organized. You can even include what days you prefer to do certain exercises or eat certain meals.
2. The best muscle building exercises involve large muscles, so make sure to include bench presses and squats in your routine.
3. If you want to grow muscle you have to increase your intake, especially protein.
4. Your biggest meal of the day should be the one after you lift weights, with about a half-hour window up to an hour.
5. Increase weight even by 1 or 2 pounds every couple of weeks or every month. Bodybuilding is a long-term investment that requires gradual increase in resistance to achieve growth and prevent injuries.
6. Perseverance is the key to achieving bodybuilding results. Stick to your goals and you will have the body you desire.
7. Warm up. Warm up. Warm up. This cannot be said enough. Don't ever jump into the heavy weights without a serious warm up.

Neglecting this tip will bring injuries that totally dismantle your training routine.

8. Muscle confusion techniques to prevent plateauing are a myth. As long as you stay motivated with your routine and keep increasing weight every 2 to 4 weeks, your bodybuilding goals will be reached.

9. Drink a lot of water during the entire day, not just around workout time. Yes, you will have a lot of bathroom interruptions but staying very well hydrated is key to muscle recovery and growth.

10. Your upper body workouts need to be well-balanced. Include all of these in your weekly routine: chest, shoulders, back, arms, and deltoids.

11. If you are very sore, do not work out that body part. Letting your body rest and avoiding injury is paramount to long-term results.

12. Try your hardest to not skip a workout, especially once you have gotten into your routine for a week or two. The initial phase is of training is steep and from there it's all about sticking to it, so don't skip the gym.

13. Alternate body parts in anticipation of workout pain. Doing chest at least a day after shoulders is better than doing it without enough rest in between as these body parts work in sync.

14. Good sleep is nearly as important as everything else. Most muscle growth and

recovery occurs while we sleep, so aiming for a restful 8 hours of sleep per day is the smart way to go.

15. Calories become muscle, but they have to be the good kind. Nuts of any kind, lots of proteins, whole-grain carbohydrates, olive oil, and avocados should be your menu.

16. Never waste a workout. If you are getting interrupted about something, either finish it and return to your routine, or completely forget about it and focus on the workout.

17. Every set, every rep counts towards muscle growth. Treat every lift and every push as the most important with good technique and your results will be dramatically better than average lifters.

18. Pushing for fatigue should be only for your very last set of that muscle group. After your fatigue set, do not go for more. It's better to rest that muscle group and prevent injury.

19. Snacking in between meals is a clever way to increase your calories. Choose nutritious snacks such as nuts, protein bars, cheeses, milk, and fruits.

20. Bench press can be difficult without a spotter. If a spotter is not around, do not push too heavy. Better be safe so you can return to the gym the next day without injuries.

21.   If you just ate and are still hungry this means your body needs more calories. GO ahead and eat more, but keep it nutritious.

22.   It's perfectly fine to go on vacation for a few days, but this should only be done after a solid routine of at least 8 weeks. This way your gains will not be lost and returning to the gym won't be as difficult.

23.   Go for strength before volume. Getting your muscles stronger at first will make it easier to push your limits and prevent injuries.

24.   Protein supplements can add valuable calories to your daily goals. Other supplements, such as creatine, carb-loaders, testosterone and energy boosters should be used with caution.

25.   Stay around motivated bodybuilders as yourself and avoid the lazy, all-talk lifters that are always late and mostly want to talk rather than workout. This will save you countless hours of valuable training.

26.   Eating soon after waking up is necessary to feed your hungry muscles after several hours of sleep. Protein with fruit and plenty of water is a good choice.

27.   Eventually you will notice a pattern: workout, eat, eat more, eat more, sleep, eat, eat more, work out, …repeat cycle. Stick to this pattern along with plenty of water, and you will see your bodybuilding goals achieved.

28. Give yourself a prize for staying true to your goals. Completely relax on your days off and do something you love.
29. Be patient. Building an amazing physique won't happen overnight. Expect results to come months at a time.
30. Pushing your limit every set, every day is neither necessary nor recommended. Better be consistent for 2 to 4 weeks before increasing weight. This way we go for strength before volume, as it should be.
31. Being sore can be predicted in two situations: when first starting an exercise and when increasing weight on the 2-4 week intervals. In between this timeframe, not being sore is normal and is a sign that your muscles are working efficiently.
32. Make your bodybuilding goals both short and long-term. Yes, you want to form muscle to last for the coming months and years, but you also want to be healthy enough to keep training into your sixties and later. Consider this with your diet and routine choices.
33. Protein should come from a variety of sources such as meat, chicken, milk, eggs, cheese, and fish.
34. When formulating a workout, be sure to prioritize larger muscle groups over smaller groups. This is a key strategy for muscle growth.

35. When mixing workouts for large muscle groups and smaller groups, always do the large group first.
36. Bigger arms are a must, so even though triceps may be boring at times, they are larger than your biceps so focus more on them.
37. Dips are a fantastic way to focus on triceps while including many muscles in one movement. If you aren't yet strong enough to a dip, then use the support available on some dip machines.
38. Chin-ups are an excellent way to boost your bicep growth while working many muscles in one movement. If you aren't yet strong enough to a chin-up, then use the support available on some chin-up machines.
39. Salt and potassium are important for muscle recovery so do not reduce or eliminate them from your diets as long as you don't suffer from hypertension, or other relevant medical conditions.
40. Cardio training is important to maintain full-body blood flow and won't hinder your muscle growth as long as you keep the cardio training light and not too intense to drain your energy or interfere with recovery.
41. Abs look great but should not be your only goal. Include your entire body in your long-term vision and you will achieve a more harmonious physique.

42. You need fats, just make sure they're the good kind. Choose from any kind of nut, avocados, and other polyunsaturated or monounsaturated kinds. Some bad fats found in junk food is ok perhaps once a week as a mischief, but these bad fats certainly should not be a regular part of your diet.

43. Always start slow when returning to your workout routine from a few days break or from longer.

44. Pace yourself. Bodybuilding is not a race, but rather a contest of perseverance and discipline.

45. Do quality sets instead of tons of reps. A set with 5 reps well-done is worth more than a dozen rep set done in a rush.

46. Avoid going too heavy or too light. Extremes are not good, as one extreme will increase your risk of injuries and the other will not build muscle. Choose a weight that is demanding but not too easy or too hard.

47. Deloading is a myth. Instead of wasting a week with very light lifting, it's better to simply rest an extra day or two and get back to your full routine.

48. Once in a while, your training routine will get off the tracks because of a variety of reasons like social events, work, injuries, traffic, among others. These things are unavoidable mostly so don't worry about it and simply get back on track with your training as soon as you are able to.

Remember to start slow whenever you had an extra day or two of rest for any reason.

49.   Enjoy the grind. Bodybuilding is a grueling and painful process that brings enormous satisfaction and pride, learn to enjoy it and your results will improve.

50.   Be proud of your perseverance and discipline. Bodybuilding is not something anyone can do. Only those with inner strength and long-term goals can choose and stick to it.

Made in the USA
Las Vegas, NV
15 September 2021

30334656R00127